Overview

"The Green Legacy: Robert F. Kennedy Jr.'s Environmental Journey" is a comprehensive and factual account of the life and accomplishments of Robert Francis Kennedy Jr. This book delves into his early life and upbringing, exploring the influence of his renowned Kennedy family legacy and the impact of family tragedies on his journey. It examines how his family played a significant role in shaping his values and beliefs, particularly in relation to environmental activism. The book extensively covers Kennedy Jr.'s environmental activism, highlighting his deep understanding of environmental issues and his early influences in this field. It explores his founding of the Waterkeeper Alliance and his involvement in environmental lawsuits and advocacy. Additionally, it delves into his notable accomplishments and contributions, including his work in environmental policy and legislation, clean energy initiatives, protection of natural resources, and promotion of sustainable practices. Furthermore, "The Green Legacy" delves into Kennedy Jr.'s beliefs and values, addressing his strong advocacy for environmental justice and equity, his views on climate change and global warming, and his concerns about corporate influence on the environment. It also explores his perspective on the murder of his father, Robert F. Kennedy, investigating the assassination, the subsequent investigations and conspiracy theories, and the profound impact it had on Kennedy Jr.'s life and career. The book also examines the opposition and controversies he has faced, including criticism of his work and challenges to environmental activism. In addition to providing an in-depth exploration of Kennedy Jr.'s life and career, the book delves into his decision to run for president in 2024. It examines his motivations, campaign platform, and policy proposals, as well as the challenges and obstacles he faced during his campaign. Furthermore, it analyzes the potential impact of his presidential run on the political landscape. "The Green Legacy" also delves into Kennedy Jr.

's personal life, including his marriage and family, personal interests and hobbies, philanthropic endeavors, and the delicate balance between his personal and professional life. It concludes by discussing his legacy and influence, examining his impact on the environmental movement, his ability to inspire future generations, and his role in continuing the Kennedy legacy. The book also reflects on the lessons learned from Kennedy Jr.'s journey, his reflections on environmental activism, personal growth and evolution, and the future challenges and opportunities that lie ahead.

Table Of Contents

1 Early Life and Family

1.1 Childhood and Upbringing

Robert Francis Kennedy Jr., commonly known as RFK Jr., was born on January 17, 1954, in Washington, D.C. He was the third of eleven children born to Robert F. Kennedy and Ethel Skakel Kennedy. Growing up in a prominent political family, RFK Jr.'s childhood and upbringing played a significant role in shaping his values, beliefs, and passion for environmental activism.

1.1.1 Early Years and Family Background

RFK Jr.'s childhood was marked by a strong sense of public service and a deep connection to his family's legacy. His father, Robert F. Kennedy, was a prominent figure in American politics, serving as the United States Attorney General and later as a U.S. Senator. His uncle, John F. Kennedy, was the 35th President of the United States.

Surrounded by such influential figures, RFK Jr. was exposed to the importance of public service and the impact individuals can have on society from an early age. His parents instilled in him a sense of duty and a commitment to fighting for justice and equality.

1.1.2 Education and Intellectual Development

RFK Jr.'s education played a crucial role in shaping his worldview and environmental consciousness. He attended the prestigious Phillips Academy in Andover, Massachusetts, where he excelled academically and developed a passion for history and literature. After graduating from Phillips Academy, he went on to study at Harvard University, where he earned a Bachelor of Arts degree in American History and Literature.

During his time at Harvard, RFK Jr. became increasingly aware of the environmental challenges facing the world. He was deeply influenced by the works of environmentalists such as Rachel Carson, whose book "Silent

Spring" exposed the harmful effects of pesticides on the environment. This exposure to environmental issues sparked his interest in conservation and set him on a path towards becoming a prominent environmental activist.

1.1.3 Family Influence and Values

RFK Jr.'s upbringing within the Kennedy family had a profound impact on his values and beliefs. The Kennedy family has a long history of public service and a commitment to social justice, which served as a guiding principle for RFK Jr. Throughout his life, he has sought to uphold the family's legacy by advocating for causes that align with his values.

The Kennedy family's commitment to public service and their dedication to fighting for the rights of the marginalized and disadvantaged influenced RFK Jr.'s decision to pursue a career in environmental activism. He saw environmental issues as interconnected with social justice, recognizing that the most vulnerable communities often bear the brunt of environmental degradation.

1.1.4 Impact of Tragedies on RFK Jr.'s Life

Tragedy struck the Kennedy family multiple times, leaving a lasting impact on RFK Jr.'s life. In 1963, when RFK Jr. was just nine years old, his uncle, President John F. Kennedy, was assassinated. This event had a profound effect on him and his family, shaping their collective understanding of the consequences of political engagement and the pursuit of justice.

Just five years later, in 1968, RFK Jr. experienced another devastating loss when his father, Robert F. Kennedy, was assassinated while running for president. The loss of his father at such a young age further fueled RFK Jr.'s determination to carry on his family's legacy and fight for the causes his father held dear.

These tragedies not only deepened RFK Jr.'s commitment to public service but also instilled in him a sense of resilience and a drive to seek justice and truth in the face of adversity.

RFK Jr.'s childhood and upbringing laid the foundation for his future endeavors as an environmental activist and shaped his unwavering commitment to fighting for a sustainable and just world. His family's influence, coupled with his personal experiences, propelled him to become a prominent voice in the environmental movement, advocating for policies that protect the planet and promote social equity.

1.2 The Kennedy Family Legacy

The Kennedy family is one of the most prominent and influential political dynasties in American history. With a legacy spanning several generations, the Kennedys have left an indelible mark on the nation's political landscape. At the forefront of this legacy is Robert Francis Kennedy Jr., the son of Senator Robert F. Kennedy and nephew of President John F. Kennedy.

The Kennedy family's commitment to public service and social justice has been a defining characteristic throughout their history. From Joseph P. Kennedy Sr., who served as the United States Ambassador to the United Kingdom, to John F. Kennedy, who became the 35th President of the United States, the Kennedys have consistently demonstrated a dedication to making a positive impact on society.

Robert F. Kennedy Jr. was born into this legacy on January 17, 1954, in Washington, D.C. As the seventh of eleven children, he grew up surrounded by a family deeply involved in politics and public service. His father, Robert F. Kennedy, served as Attorney General under President John F. Kennedy and later as a U.S. Senator from New York.

The Kennedy family's commitment to social justice and civil rights deeply influenced Robert F. Kennedy Jr. from an early age. He witnessed firsthand the struggles and triumphs of his father and uncle as they fought for equality and justice for all Americans. Their dedication to public service and their unwavering belief in the power of government to effect positive change left an indelible impression on him.

Tragically, the Kennedy family also experienced profound personal losses that shaped Robert F. Kennedy Jr.'s worldview. The assassinations of his uncle, President John F. Kennedy, in 1963, and his father, Senator Robert F. Kennedy, in 1968, had a profound impact on him and his family. These tragic events not only shaped his understanding of the world but also fueled his determination to carry on their legacy of public service and social justice.

The Kennedy family's commitment to public service and their belief in the power of government to effect positive change have been instrumental in shaping Robert F. Kennedy Jr.'s career and activism. He has often spoken about the influence his family has had on his life, emphasizing the importance of their values and principles in guiding his own actions.

Robert F. Kennedy Jr.'s environmental activism can be seen as an extension of the Kennedy family's commitment to social justice. He has often cited his family's legacy as a driving force behind his dedication to protecting the environment and advocating for sustainable practices. In his work, he seeks to honor the values instilled in him by his family and to continue their legacy of making a positive impact on society.

While the Kennedy family legacy has provided Robert F. Kennedy Jr. with a strong foundation and a sense of purpose, it has also brought its share of challenges. As a member of such a prominent family, he has faced scrutiny and criticism from those who oppose his views and beliefs. However, he has remained steadfast in his convictions, using his platform to advocate for environmental justice and equity.

In conclusion, the Kennedy family legacy has played a significant role in shaping Robert F. Kennedy Jr.'s life and career. From his upbringing in a family dedicated to public service to the tragic losses that fueled his determination, the Kennedy family's influence is evident in his activism and advocacy. As he continues to carry on their legacy, Robert F. Kennedy Jr. remains committed to making a positive impact on the world and inspiring future generations to do the same.

1.3 Family Tragedies and Their Impact

The Kennedy family has been marked by a series of tragic events that have had a profound impact on the lives of its members, including Robert F. Kennedy Jr. These family tragedies have shaped his worldview, influenced his career choices, and fueled his passion for justice and activism.

One of the most devastating events in the Kennedy family's history was the assassination of Robert F. Kennedy Sr., the father of Robert F. Kennedy Jr. On June 5, 1968, while running for the presidency, Robert F. Kennedy Sr. was shot and killed at the Ambassador Hotel in Los Angeles. This tragic event not only robbed the nation of a potential leader but also left a lasting impact on the Kennedy family, particularly on young Robert Jr., who was only 14 years old at the time.

The loss of his father had a profound effect on Robert F. Kennedy Jr. It ignited a deep sense of loss, grief, and a desire for justice. In the aftermath of his father's assassination, Robert Jr. became determined to carry on his father's legacy and fight for the causes his father held dear. This tragic event served as a catalyst for his lifelong commitment to public service and activism.

Unfortunately, the Kennedy family was no stranger to tragedy. Prior to the assassination of Robert F. Kennedy Sr., the family had already experienced the loss of President John F. Kennedy, Robert Jr.'s uncle, who was assassinated in 1963. These two assassinations within a span of five years left an indelible mark on the Kennedy family and shaped their collective identity as a family dedicated to public service and social justice.

The impact of these family tragedies on Robert F. Kennedy Jr. cannot be overstated. They instilled in him a deep sense of responsibility to carry on the family's legacy and fight for the causes his father and uncle believed in. The loss of his father and uncle at such young ages also made him acutely aware of the fragility of life and the importance of making a positive impact while he had the opportunity.

In addition to the assassinations of his father and uncle, Robert F. Kennedy Jr. has also faced personal tragedies within his immediate family. In 1984, his brother David Kennedy died of a drug overdose, further deepening the family's grief and loss. These personal tragedies have undoubtedly shaped Robert Jr.'s perspective on addiction and mental health, leading him to advocate for better treatment and support systems for those struggling with these issues.

Despite the immense pain and loss experienced by the Kennedy family, they have managed to find strength and resilience in the face of adversity. Robert F. Kennedy Jr., in particular, has channeled his grief into a lifelong commitment to fighting for justice, protecting the environment, and advocating for the most vulnerable members of society.

The family tragedies have also served as a source of inspiration for Robert Jr. He has often spoken about the impact his father's death had on his own life and how it motivated him to make a difference in the world. He has dedicated himself to carrying on his father's legacy and ensuring that his work and ideals are not forgotten.

The family tragedies have also made Robert F. Kennedy Jr. acutely aware of the dangers and consequences of political violence. He has been a vocal critic of violence as a means of achieving political goals and has called for peaceful and nonviolent methods of bringing about social change.

In conclusion, the family tragedies experienced by the Kennedy family, including the assassinations of Robert F. Kennedy Sr. and President John F. Kennedy, as well as the personal loss of Robert Jr.'s brother, have had a profound impact on Robert F. Kennedy Jr.'s life and career. These tragedies have shaped his worldview, fueled his passion for justice and activism, and inspired him to carry on the family's legacy of public service. Despite the immense pain and loss, Robert Jr. has emerged as a resilient advocate for social justice, environmental protection, and the pursuit of truth.

13

1.4 Influence of Family on Robert F. Kennedy Jr.

Robert F. Kennedy Jr. was born into one of America's most prominent political families, and the influence of his family played a significant role in shaping his values, beliefs, and career path. As the son of Senator Robert F. Kennedy and nephew of President John F. Kennedy, he grew up surrounded by a legacy of public service and a commitment to social justice.

From an early age, Robert F. Kennedy Jr. was exposed to the ideals and principles that his family held dear. His father, Senator Robert F. Kennedy, was a champion of civil rights and a vocal advocate for the marginalized and oppressed. He fought tirelessly for equality and justice, and his passion for making a positive impact on the world left a lasting impression on his son.

The Kennedy family's commitment to public service and their dedication to fighting for the rights of others instilled in Robert F. Kennedy Jr. a deep sense of responsibility and a desire to make a difference. He witnessed firsthand the power of using one's privilege and influence to effect change, and he was inspired to follow in his family's footsteps.

Growing up in such a politically active and socially conscious environment, Robert F. Kennedy Jr. was exposed to a wide range of perspectives and ideas. Dinner table conversations often revolved around important issues of the day, and he was encouraged to think critically and form his own opinions. This upbringing fostered in him a strong sense of social justice and a commitment to fighting for the rights of the voiceless.

The tragic loss of his father at a young age had a profound impact on Robert F. Kennedy Jr. and further fueled his determination to carry on his family's legacy. The assassination of Senator Robert F. Kennedy in 1968 was a devastating blow to the Kennedy family and the nation as a whole. It was a moment that forever changed the course of history and shaped the trajectory of Robert F. Kennedy Jr.'s life.

The murder of his father not only deepened his commitment to social justice but also fueled his desire to seek truth and justice. Over the years, Robert F. Kennedy Jr. has been outspoken about his views on the assassination, advocating for a thorough investigation and challenging the official narrative. He has tirelessly sought answers and has been a vocal critic of the shortcomings of the investigation.

Despite facing opposition and criticism for his views, Robert F. Kennedy Jr. remains steadfast in his pursuit of justice for his father. He believes that the full truth surrounding the assassination has yet to be uncovered and continues to advocate for a comprehensive reexamination of the case.

In addition to the influence of his family, Robert F. Kennedy Jr. has also been shaped by his own personal experiences and the challenges he has faced throughout his life. His struggles with addiction and his journey towards recovery have given him a unique perspective on the issues of mental health and substance abuse. These experiences have further fueled his passion for advocating for those who are marginalized and underserved.

While Robert F. Kennedy Jr. has faced opposition and controversy throughout his career, he remains committed to his beliefs and principles. His outspoken nature and willingness to challenge the status quo have made him a polarizing figure in the environmental and political spheres. However, he continues to use his platform to raise awareness about important issues and to advocate for change.

As Robert F. Kennedy Jr. embarks on his presidential campaign in 2024, his family's influence will undoubtedly play a significant role in shaping his platform and policy proposals. The Kennedy legacy of public service and social justice will continue to guide his vision for a better future.

In conclusion, the influence of family on Robert F. Kennedy Jr. cannot be overstated. From his upbringing in a politically active and socially conscious environment to the tragic loss of his father, his family's values and experiences have shaped his beliefs, his commitment to justice, and his determination to make a positive impact on the world. As he continues to navigate the challenges and opportunities that lie ahead, his family's legacy will remain a driving force in his journey.

2 Environmental Activism

2.1 Introduction to Environmental Issues

Environmental issues have become increasingly prominent in recent years, as the world grapples with the consequences of human activities on the planet. Robert F. Kennedy Jr., an influential environmental activist, has dedicated his life to raising awareness about these issues and advocating for sustainable practices. In this section, we will explore Kennedy's introduction to environmental issues and the factors that shaped his passion for environmental activism.

Kennedy's journey into environmental activism began with a deep concern for the well-being of the natural world. Growing up in a family that valued public service and social justice, he was instilled with a sense of responsibility to protect the environment. As a child, Kennedy spent summers exploring the natural beauty of the Kennedy family compound in Hyannis Port, Massachusetts. These experiences fostered a deep connection to nature and a desire to preserve it for future generations.

In his early years, Kennedy witnessed the devastating effects of pollution and environmental degradation firsthand. He observed the decline of fish populations and the pollution of rivers and lakes near his childhood home. These experiences ignited a passion within him to take action and fight for environmental conservation.

Kennedy's environmental awakening was further fueled by his education. He studied at Harvard University, where he delved into the fields of environmental science and law. This interdisciplinary approach allowed him to understand the complex relationship between human activities and the environment. It also equipped him with the knowledge and tools necessary to advocate for environmental protection.

One of the key turning points in Kennedy's environmental journey was the founding of the Waterkeeper Alliance in 1999. Inspired by his father's commitment to social justice, Kennedy joined forces with environmental attorney John H. Adams to establish this global movement dedicated to protecting waterways and ensuring clean water for all. The Waterkeeper Alliance empowers local communities to take action against polluters and holds corporations accountable for their environmental impact.

Kennedy's environmental activism also extends to his involvement in numerous lawsuits and advocacy efforts. He has been at the forefront of legal battles against corporations and government entities that prioritize profit over environmental sustainability. Through his work as an attorney, Kennedy has fought to enforce environmental laws and regulations, ensuring that polluters are held accountable for their actions.

Moreover, Kennedy has been a vocal advocate for renewable energy and clean technologies. He recognizes the urgent need to transition away from fossil fuels and embrace sustainable alternatives to mitigate the impacts of climate change. Through his advocacy and public speaking engagements, Kennedy has raised awareness about the importance of investing in clean energy initiatives and reducing greenhouse gas emissions.

Kennedy's environmental activism is deeply rooted in his beliefs and values. He firmly believes in the principles of environmental justice and equity, advocating for equal access to clean air, water, and a healthy environment for all communities, regardless of socioeconomic status or race. He recognizes that marginalized communities often bear the brunt of environmental pollution and fights for their rights to a safe and healthy environment.

Furthermore, Kennedy has been a staunch critic of corporate influence on the environment. He has spoken out against the undue influence of powerful industries that prioritize profit over the well-being of the planet. Kennedy believes that corporate accountability is essential for achieving sustainable and equitable environmental policies.

Kennedy's outspoken views on the murder of his father, Senator Robert F. Kennedy, have also shaped his environmental activism. He has been a vocal advocate for justice and truth, tirelessly seeking answers and challenging official narratives surrounding his father's assassination. This pursuit of justice has fueled his commitment to fighting for a more just and equitable society, including environmental justice.

However, Kennedy's environmental activism has not been without opposition and controversy. Critics have questioned his motives and accused him of spreading misinformation. Some have even targeted him personally, attempting to discredit his work and tarnish his reputation. Despite these challenges, Kennedy has remained steadfast in his commitment to environmental advocacy, using evidence-based research and scientific expertise to debunk falsehoods and promote informed dialogue.

Looking ahead, Kennedy's run for President in 2024 represents a significant milestone in his environmental journey. Motivated by a desire to bring about meaningful change on a national scale, he has outlined a comprehensive campaign platform focused on environmental sustainability, social justice, and public health. His candidacy has sparked both enthusiasm and skepticism, highlighting the polarizing nature of environmental issues in today's political landscape.

In conclusion, Robert F. Kennedy Jr.'s introduction to environmental issues was shaped by his upbringing, education, and personal experiences. His passion for environmental activism is rooted in a deep concern for the well-being of the planet and a commitment to social justice. Through his work with organizations like the Waterkeeper Alliance and his advocacy efforts, Kennedy has made significant contributions to the environmental movement. Despite facing opposition and controversy, he remains dedicated to fighting for a more sustainable and equitable future.

2.2 Early Environmental Influences

Robert F. Kennedy Jr.'s passion for environmental activism can be traced back to his early years and the influences he encountered during his upbringing. Growing up in a prominent political family, Kennedy was exposed to a wide range of experiences and individuals who shaped his perspective on environmental issues.

2.2.1 Childhood Experiences in Nature

As a child, Robert F. Kennedy Jr. spent a significant amount of time outdoors, exploring the natural world around him. He developed a deep appreciation for the beauty and wonder of nature, which laid the foundation for his later environmental advocacy. Whether it was hiking in the mountains, swimming in rivers, or observing wildlife, these experiences instilled in him a sense of awe and respect for the environment.

2.2.2 Family Influence

Growing up as part of the Kennedy family, Robert F. Kennedy Jr. was surrounded by individuals who were deeply committed to public service and social justice. His father, Robert F. Kennedy, and his uncle, President John F. Kennedy, were influential figures who championed causes related to civil rights, poverty alleviation, and international diplomacy. Their commitment to making a positive impact on society undoubtedly influenced Kennedy's own desire to effect change.

2.2.3 Mentorship from Family Members

In addition to the broader influence of his family, Robert F. Kennedy Jr. received direct mentorship from family members who were actively involved in environmental issues. His aunt, Eunice Kennedy Shriver, was a passionate advocate for people with intellectual disabilities and founded the Special Olympics. Her dedication to social justice and inclusivity inspired

Kennedy to consider the interconnectedness of environmental issues with broader societal concerns.

2.2.4 Exposure to Environmental Issues

During his formative years, Robert F. Kennedy Jr. was exposed to various environmental issues through his family's travels and experiences. He witnessed firsthand the devastating effects of pollution and environmental degradation in different parts of the world. These experiences deepened his understanding of the urgent need for environmental conservation and motivated him to take action.

2.2.5 Education and Academic Influences

Robert F. Kennedy Jr.'s academic pursuits further shaped his environmental consciousness. He studied at Harvard University, where he earned a degree in American History and Literature. During his time at Harvard, Kennedy became involved in environmental activism and joined the Harvard Environmental Law Review. This experience allowed him to delve deeper into the legal and policy aspects of environmental protection.

2.2.6 Mentorship from Environmental Leaders

Throughout his journey, Robert F. Kennedy Jr. had the privilege of learning from and working alongside influential environmental leaders. One of his most significant mentors was William K. Reilly, the former head of the Environmental Protection Agency (EPA). Reilly's guidance and expertise helped Kennedy develop a comprehensive understanding of environmental policy and the importance of collaboration between government agencies and grassroots organizations.

2.2.7 Personal Experiences with Environmental Injustice

Robert F. Kennedy Jr.'s early environmental influences were also shaped by personal experiences with environmental injustice. He witnessed the detrimental impact of pollution on marginalized communities, particularly those living in poverty. These experiences fueled his commitment to fighting for environmental justice and ensuring that all individuals, regardless of their socioeconomic status, have access to clean air, water, and a healthy environment.

2.2.8 The Influence of Rachel Carson's "Silent Spring"

Another significant influence on Robert F. Kennedy Jr.'s environmental journey was the groundbreaking book "Silent Spring" by Rachel Carson. This seminal work, which exposed the harmful effects of pesticides on the environment and human health, had a profound impact on Kennedy's understanding of the interconnectedness between human activities and the natural world. Carson's work inspired him to advocate for the protection of ecosystems and the promotion of sustainable practices.

In conclusion, Robert F. Kennedy Jr.'s early environmental influences were diverse and multifaceted. From his childhood experiences in nature to the mentorship he received from family members and environmental leaders, these influences shaped his passion for environmental activism. Through personal experiences and exposure to environmental issues, Kennedy developed a deep understanding of the urgent need for environmental conservation and justice. These early influences laid the foundation for his future accomplishments and contributions to the field of environmental advocacy.

2.3 Founding of Waterkeeper Alliance

In his ongoing commitment to environmental activism, Robert F. Kennedy Jr. played a pivotal role in the founding of the Waterkeeper Alliance. This organization has become a powerful force in protecting and preserving waterways around the world. Kennedy's involvement in the creation of the Waterkeeper Alliance showcases his dedication to safeguarding our natural resources and ensuring clean water for future generations.

The Need for Waterkeeper Alliance

Recognizing the urgent need to address the deteriorating state of our waterways, Kennedy joined forces with environmental attorney and activist John H. Adams in 1999. Together, they established the Waterkeeper Alliance, a global movement dedicated to protecting and restoring the world's water bodies. The organization's mission is to champion the rights of communities to clean water and to hold polluters accountable for their actions.

The Role of Waterkeepers

At the heart of the Waterkeeper Alliance are the Waterkeepers themselves. These dedicated individuals, often local activists, serve as the eyes and ears of their communities, monitoring and protecting their respective water bodies. Waterkeepers are committed to upholding the principles of environmental justice and ensuring that everyone has access to clean and safe water.

Building a Global Network

One of the key achievements of the Waterkeeper Alliance is its ability to build a vast network of organizations and individuals working towards a common goal. By connecting local Waterkeepers and supporting their efforts, the Alliance has created a powerful collective voice for water protection. This network spans over 350 Waterkeeper organizations in more than 40 countries, making it one of the largest and most influential environmental movements in the world.

Advocacy and Legal Action

The Waterkeeper Alliance is not only focused on monitoring and reporting pollution but also on taking legal action against those who violate environmental regulations. Through strategic litigation, the Alliance has successfully held corporations and government entities accountable for their actions, resulting in significant victories for water protection. These legal battles have not only resulted in cleaner water but have also set important precedents for environmental law.

Collaborations and Partnerships

Recognizing the importance of collaboration, the Waterkeeper Alliance actively seeks partnerships with other organizations, government agencies, and individuals who share their commitment to water protection. By working together, they can amplify their impact and create lasting change. These collaborations have led to innovative solutions, such as the development of sustainable practices and the implementation of effective pollution control measures.

Education and Outreach

In addition to their advocacy and legal efforts, the Waterkeeper Alliance places great emphasis on education and outreach. They believe that raising awareness and empowering communities is crucial in creating a sustainable future. Through educational programs, public events, and community engagement, the Alliance strives to inspire individuals to take action and become stewards of their local waterways.

Impact and Recognition

Since its inception, the Waterkeeper Alliance has made significant strides in protecting and restoring water bodies worldwide. Their work has resulted in the cleanup of polluted rivers, the prevention of harmful industrial practices, and the preservation of fragile ecosystems. The Alliance's efforts have been widely recognized, and they have received numerous awards and accolades for their contributions to environmental conservation.

Kennedy's Role and Influence

As one of the co-founders of the Waterkeeper Alliance, Robert F. Kennedy Jr. played a crucial role in shaping the organization's vision and mission. His passion for environmental justice and his expertise in environmental law have been instrumental in guiding the Alliance's strategies and initiatives. Kennedy's involvement has also brought significant attention and support to the cause, helping to raise awareness and mobilize resources.

Through the founding of the Waterkeeper Alliance, Robert F. Kennedy Jr. has demonstrated his unwavering commitment to protecting our water resources. His efforts have not only resulted in tangible improvements in water quality but have also inspired countless individuals to take action and become advocates for environmental conservation. The Waterkeeper Alliance stands as a testament to Kennedy's enduring legacy and his dedication to creating a sustainable and just future for all.

2.4 Environmental Lawsuits and Advocacy

Robert F. Kennedy Jr.'s commitment to environmental activism extends beyond founding organizations and advocating for clean water. Throughout his career, he has been involved in numerous environmental lawsuits and has used his legal expertise to fight for the protection of natural resources and the promotion of sustainable practices. This section explores some of the significant environmental lawsuits and advocacy efforts undertaken by Robert F. Kennedy Jr.

2.4.1 Lawsuits against Polluters

One of the key aspects of Robert F. Kennedy Jr.'s environmental advocacy has been his involvement in lawsuits against polluters. Recognizing that legal action can be a powerful tool to hold corporations accountable for their environmental impact, Kennedy has taken on several high-profile cases. He has represented communities affected by pollution, seeking justice for those whose health and well-being have been compromised by industrial activities.

Kennedy's legal battles have targeted industries such as coal mining, oil and gas, and chemical manufacturing. By taking on these cases, he has sought to expose the harmful practices of these industries and push for stricter regulations to protect the environment and public health. His efforts have resulted in significant victories, leading to improved environmental standards and increased corporate responsibility.

2.4.2 Advocacy for Clean Energy

Recognizing the urgent need to transition to clean and renewable energy sources, Robert F. Kennedy Jr. has been a vocal advocate for clean energy initiatives. He has consistently championed the development and implementation of renewable energy technologies as a means to combat climate change and reduce dependence on fossil fuels.

Kennedy has been involved in legal battles to promote clean energy, including advocating for the expansion of wind and solar power. He has fought against the construction of fossil fuel infrastructure, such as pipelines and coal-fired power plants, and has instead advocated for the adoption of sustainable alternatives. Through his advocacy, Kennedy has played a crucial role in shaping policies and legislation that support the growth of clean energy industries.

2.4.3 Protection of Public Lands and Wildlife

Robert F. Kennedy Jr. has been a staunch defender of public lands and wildlife conservation. He has actively fought against the exploitation of natural resources and the destruction of ecosystems. Kennedy has been involved in lawsuits to protect national parks, wildlife refuges, and other environmentally sensitive areas from harmful development and industrial activities.

His advocacy efforts have focused on preserving biodiversity, protecting endangered species, and ensuring the sustainable management of natural resources. Kennedy has worked closely with environmental organizations and local communities to challenge projects that threaten the integrity of ecosystems and disrupt the balance of nature. Through his legal expertise and environmental knowledge, he has been instrumental in safeguarding precious habitats for future generations.

2.4.4 Environmental Policy and Legislative Advocacy

In addition to his involvement in lawsuits, Robert F. Kennedy Jr. has been actively engaged in shaping environmental policy and advocating for legislative changes. He has worked closely with lawmakers and policymakers to develop and promote legislation that addresses pressing environmental issues.

Kennedy's advocacy efforts have focused on a wide range of environmental concerns, including water pollution, air quality, climate change, and the protection of natural resources. He has testified before Congress, provided expert advice to government agencies, and collaborated with environmental organizations to draft and support legislation that advances environmental protection and sustainability.

Through his lawsuits and advocacy work, Robert F. Kennedy Jr. has demonstrated his unwavering commitment to environmental justice and the preservation of our planet. His legal expertise, combined with his passion for the environment, has made him a formidable force in the fight against environmental degradation. Kennedy's efforts have not only resulted in tangible victories but have also inspired countless individuals to take action and join the movement for a greener and more sustainable future.

3 Accomplishments and Contributions

3.1 Environmental Policy and Legislation

Robert F. Kennedy Jr. has been a prominent figure in the field of environmental policy and legislation. Throughout his career, he has played a crucial role in shaping environmental laws and advocating for their implementation. His dedication to protecting the environment and promoting sustainable practices has made a significant impact on the global environmental movement.

3.1.1 Advocacy for Strong Environmental Laws

One of the key aspects of Robert F. Kennedy Jr.'s environmental journey has been his advocacy for strong environmental laws. He firmly believes that robust legislation is essential for safeguarding the environment and ensuring a sustainable future for generations to come. Kennedy has been actively involved in the drafting and promotion of various environmental laws at both the state and federal levels.

Kennedy's work has focused on addressing critical environmental issues such as water pollution, air pollution, and the protection of natural resources. He has been a vocal advocate for the enforcement of existing laws and the creation of new legislation to address emerging environmental challenges. His efforts have led to the strengthening of environmental regulations and the establishment of stricter standards for industries and individuals alike.

3.1.2 The Clean Water Act and Waterkeeper Alliance

One of the most significant contributions of Robert F. Kennedy Jr. to environmental policy is his involvement in the creation of the Waterkeeper Alliance. Inspired by his father's commitment to public service, Kennedy co-founded the organization in 1999. The Waterkeeper Alliance is a global movement dedicated to protecting and preserving water resources.

Under Kennedy's leadership, the Waterkeeper Alliance has grown into a powerful force for environmental advocacy. The organization works to ensure the enforcement of the Clean Water Act, a landmark legislation passed in 1972. Kennedy has been instrumental in raising awareness about the importance of clean water and the need for strong regulations to prevent water pollution.

Through the Waterkeeper Alliance, Kennedy has supported local communities in their efforts to monitor and protect their waterways. The organization has filed numerous lawsuits against polluters and has successfully held corporations accountable for their actions. Kennedy's work with the Waterkeeper Alliance has been instrumental in promoting clean water initiatives and inspiring others to take action.

3.1.3 The Endangered Species Act and Habitat Protection

Another area where Robert F. Kennedy Jr. has made significant contributions is in the protection of endangered species and their habitats. He has been a staunch advocate for the enforcement and strengthening of the Endangered Species Act, a critical piece of legislation enacted in 1973.

Kennedy believes that protecting biodiversity is essential for maintaining the health and balance of ecosystems. He has worked tirelessly to raise awareness about the importance of preserving habitats and preventing the extinction of endangered species. Through his advocacy, Kennedy has helped secure the designation of critical habitats and has fought against projects that would harm vulnerable ecosystems.

3.1.4 Climate Change Mitigation and Renewable Energy

Recognizing the urgent need to address climate change, Robert F. Kennedy Jr. has been a vocal proponent of clean and renewable energy sources. He has advocated for the transition from fossil fuels to sustainable alternatives, such as wind, solar, and geothermal energy.

Kennedy has been involved in promoting clean energy initiatives and has supported policies that incentivize the development and adoption of renewable technologies. He has emphasized the importance of reducing greenhouse gas emissions and has called for international cooperation to combat climate change.

Additionally, Kennedy has been a strong advocate for energy efficiency measures and the promotion of sustainable practices in various sectors, including transportation and agriculture. He believes that a comprehensive approach is necessary to mitigate the impacts of climate change and ensure a sustainable future for all.

In conclusion, Robert F. Kennedy Jr.'s environmental policy and legislative efforts have been instrumental in shaping the environmental movement. His advocacy for strong environmental laws, his work with the Waterkeeper Alliance, his efforts to protect endangered species and their habitats, and his promotion of clean energy initiatives have made a lasting impact on environmental policy and legislation. Kennedy's dedication to environmental protection continues to inspire and drive positive change in the fight against climate change and the preservation of our natural resources.

3.2 Clean Energy Initiatives

Clean energy initiatives have been at the forefront of Robert F. Kennedy Jr.'s environmental journey. Recognizing the urgent need to transition away from fossil fuels and reduce greenhouse gas emissions, Kennedy has been a vocal advocate for clean and renewable energy sources. Through his work and activism, he has made significant contributions to the promotion and implementation of clean energy initiatives.

3.2.1 Promoting Renewable Energy Sources

One of the key aspects of Kennedy's clean energy initiatives is the promotion of renewable energy sources. He has been a strong proponent of harnessing the power of wind, solar, and hydroelectric energy to meet our energy needs while minimizing the environmental impact. Kennedy believes that investing in renewable energy is not only crucial for combating climate change but also for creating jobs and stimulating economic growth.

Kennedy has actively supported the development and expansion of wind farms and solar power plants across the United States. He has advocated for policies and incentives that encourage the adoption of renewable energy technologies, such as tax credits for renewable energy projects and net metering programs. By promoting the use of clean and sustainable energy sources, Kennedy aims to reduce our dependence on fossil fuels and mitigate the harmful effects of climate change.

3.2.2 Advancing Energy Efficiency

In addition to promoting renewable energy sources, Kennedy has emphasized the importance of energy efficiency in reducing greenhouse gas emissions. He believes that improving energy efficiency is a cost-effective way to address climate change and reduce our carbon footprint. Kennedy has been a strong advocate for energy-efficient building practices, including the use of energy-saving technologies and materials.

Kennedy has supported initiatives that encourage the retrofitting of existing buildings to improve energy efficiency and the implementation of stricter energy efficiency standards for new construction. He has also called for increased investment in research and development of energy-efficient technologies and the adoption of energy-saving practices in industries and households.

3.2.3 Supporting Clean Transportation

Recognizing the significant contribution of the transportation sector to greenhouse gas emissions, Kennedy has been a vocal supporter of clean transportation initiatives. He has advocated for the development and adoption of electric vehicles (EVs) as a means to reduce carbon emissions from the transportation sector.

Kennedy has called for the expansion of EV charging infrastructure and the implementation of policies that incentivize the purchase and use of electric vehicles. He believes that transitioning to electric transportation is not only essential for reducing air pollution and mitigating climate change but also for reducing our dependence on fossil fuels and promoting energy independence.

3.2.4 Collaborating with Businesses and Governments

Kennedy understands that addressing the challenges of clean energy requires collaboration between various stakeholders, including businesses and governments. He has worked closely with companies and organizations to promote clean energy initiatives and encourage sustainable practices.

Kennedy has collaborated with businesses to develop and implement renewable energy projects, such as solar installations and wind farms. He has also engaged with government officials and policymakers to advocate for the adoption of clean energy policies and regulations. By fostering partnerships and alliances, Kennedy aims to create a supportive environment for clean

energy initiatives and drive the transition to a sustainable and low-carbon
future.

3.2.5 Educating and Raising Awareness

In addition to his advocacy and activism, Kennedy has played a crucial role in
educating the public about the importance of clean energy and its benefits. He
has delivered numerous speeches, lectures, and presentations to raise
awareness about the need for clean energy initiatives and the potential of
renewable energy sources.

Kennedy has also written extensively on the subject, publishing articles and
books that highlight the environmental and economic advantages of clean
energy. Through his educational efforts, he aims to inspire individuals and
communities to take action and support clean energy initiatives in their own
lives and communities.

In conclusion, Robert F. Kennedy Jr. has been a tireless advocate for clean
energy initiatives. Through his promotion of renewable energy sources,
advancement of energy efficiency, support for clean transportation,
collaboration with businesses and governments, and educational efforts,
Kennedy has made significant contributions to the transition towards a
sustainable and clean energy future. His work and dedication have not only
helped combat climate change but also inspired others to take action and make
a positive impact on the environment.

3.3 Protection of Natural Resources

Robert F. Kennedy Jr. has been a staunch advocate for the protection of natural resources throughout his career. Recognizing the importance of preserving our environment for future generations, he has dedicated himself to fighting for the conservation and sustainable management of our planet's precious resources.

3.3.1 Conservation Efforts

One of the key aspects of Kennedy's work in protecting natural resources has been his focus on conservation efforts. He understands that the responsible use and preservation of our natural resources are essential for maintaining the delicate balance of ecosystems and ensuring the long-term sustainability of our planet.

Kennedy has been actively involved in promoting the conservation of forests, rivers, and oceans. He has worked tirelessly to raise awareness about the importance of preserving these ecosystems and has been instrumental in establishing protected areas and wildlife sanctuaries. By advocating for the conservation of these natural resources, Kennedy aims to safeguard biodiversity and maintain the ecological balance necessary for the survival of countless species.

3.3.2 Water Conservation

Water is one of the most vital natural resources, and Kennedy has been a leading voice in advocating for its conservation. As the founder of the Waterkeeper Alliance, he has been at the forefront of efforts to protect and restore the world's waterways. The organization works to ensure that water bodies are free from pollution and are accessible to all.

Kennedy's commitment to water conservation extends beyond advocacy. He has actively participated in clean-up initiatives and has been involved in legal battles to hold polluters accountable for their actions. By championing the protection of water resources, Kennedy aims to secure clean and safe drinking water for communities and preserve the health of aquatic ecosystems.

3.3.3 Preservation of Land and Wildlife

Preserving land and protecting wildlife habitats are crucial components of Kennedy's efforts to safeguard natural resources. He recognizes the importance of maintaining the integrity of ecosystems and the need to protect endangered species from extinction.

Kennedy has been involved in numerous initiatives aimed at preserving land and creating wildlife corridors to ensure the free movement of animals. He has also been a vocal advocate for the protection of national parks and other protected areas. By working to preserve these natural spaces, Kennedy aims to maintain biodiversity, protect fragile ecosystems, and provide future generations with the opportunity to experience the wonders of nature.

3.3.4 Sustainable Agriculture and Fishing

Recognizing the impact of agriculture and fishing on natural resources, Kennedy has been a strong proponent of sustainable practices in these industries. He believes that it is possible to meet our food needs while minimizing the negative environmental consequences associated with conventional farming and fishing methods.

Kennedy has been actively involved in promoting organic farming and supporting small-scale farmers who prioritize sustainable practices. He has also advocated for responsible fishing practices that protect marine ecosystems and ensure the long-term viability of fish stocks. By championing sustainable agriculture and fishing, Kennedy aims to reduce the environmental footprint of these industries and promote a more harmonious relationship between humans and nature.

3.3.5 Renewable Energy and Resource Efficiency

In addition to protecting natural resources, Kennedy has been a strong advocate for clean and renewable energy sources. He recognizes the urgent need to transition away from fossil fuels and embrace sustainable alternatives to mitigate the impacts of climate change.

Kennedy has been involved in promoting renewable energy projects and advocating for policies that support their development. He believes that investing in clean energy not only helps protect natural resources but also creates jobs and stimulates economic growth. Furthermore, he has emphasized the importance of resource efficiency, encouraging individuals and businesses to reduce waste and adopt sustainable practices.

By promoting renewable energy and resource efficiency, Kennedy aims to reduce our dependence on finite resources, mitigate climate change, and create a more sustainable future for generations to come.

In conclusion, Robert F. Kennedy Jr. has made significant contributions to the protection of natural resources throughout his career. His efforts in conservation, water protection, land preservation, sustainable agriculture, and renewable energy have had a lasting impact on the environmental movement. By advocating for the responsible use and preservation of our planet's resources, Kennedy has demonstrated his commitment to creating a more sustainable and resilient future.

3.4 Promotion of Sustainable Practices

Robert F. Kennedy Jr. has been a vocal advocate for promoting sustainable practices as a means to address the pressing environmental challenges facing our planet. Throughout his career, he has worked tirelessly to raise awareness about the importance of adopting sustainable practices in various sectors, including energy, agriculture, transportation, and waste management. Kennedy firmly believes that by embracing sustainable practices, we can mitigate the impacts of climate change, protect our natural resources, and create a healthier and more equitable future for all.

3.4.1 Sustainable Energy Solutions

One of the key areas where Robert F. Kennedy Jr. has focused his efforts is in promoting sustainable energy solutions. He recognizes the urgent need to transition away from fossil fuels and towards renewable sources of energy. Kennedy has been a strong proponent of investing in clean energy technologies such as solar, wind, and geothermal power. He believes that by harnessing the power of these renewable resources, we can reduce greenhouse gas emissions, combat climate change, and create new job opportunities in the green energy sector.

Kennedy has also been a vocal critic of the influence of the fossil fuel industry on government policies and has advocated for the removal of subsidies and tax breaks for these industries. He believes that by leveling the playing field and providing incentives for renewable energy development, we can accelerate the transition to a sustainable energy future.

3.4.2 Sustainable Agriculture and Food Systems

In addition to promoting sustainable energy solutions, Robert F. Kennedy Jr. has been a strong advocate for sustainable agriculture and food systems. He recognizes the significant environmental impacts of industrial agriculture, including deforestation, water pollution, and greenhouse gas emissions. Kennedy has been a vocal supporter of organic farming practices, regenerative agriculture, and the promotion of local and sustainable food systems.

Kennedy believes that by adopting sustainable agricultural practices, we can protect soil health, conserve water resources, and reduce the use of harmful pesticides and synthetic fertilizers. He has been actively involved in supporting initiatives that promote organic farming and sustainable food production, including advocating for stricter regulations on genetically modified organisms (GMOs) and the labeling of genetically engineered foods.

3.4.3 Sustainable Transportation and Infrastructure

Another area where Robert F. Kennedy Jr. has focused his efforts is in promoting sustainable transportation and infrastructure. He recognizes the significant contribution of the transportation sector to greenhouse gas emissions and air pollution. Kennedy has been a strong advocate for investing in public transportation, promoting electric vehicles, and improving the efficiency of our transportation systems.

Kennedy believes that by expanding public transportation options, investing in clean and efficient technologies, and promoting alternative modes of transportation such as biking and walking, we can reduce our dependence on fossil fuels and create more livable and sustainable communities. He has also been a vocal critic of projects that contribute to urban sprawl and the destruction of natural habitats, advocating for smart growth and sustainable urban planning.

3.4.4 Waste Management and Recycling

Robert F. Kennedy Jr. has also been a staunch advocate for sustainable waste management and recycling practices. He recognizes the environmental and health impacts of improper waste disposal and the need to reduce waste generation and promote recycling. Kennedy has been actively involved in supporting initiatives that promote waste reduction, recycling, and the development of sustainable waste management systems.

Kennedy believes that by implementing comprehensive recycling programs, promoting the use of recycled materials, and reducing the generation of single-use plastics, we can minimize the environmental impacts of waste and move towards a circular economy. He has also been a vocal critic of the disposal of hazardous waste in marginalized communities, advocating for environmental justice and equitable waste management practices.

In conclusion, Robert F. Kennedy Jr. has been a tireless advocate for promoting sustainable practices in various sectors. Through his work, he has raised awareness about the importance of adopting sustainable energy solutions, promoting sustainable agriculture and food systems, improving sustainable transportation and infrastructure, and implementing sustainable waste management practices. Kennedy's efforts have not only contributed to the protection of our environment but also to the creation of a more sustainable and equitable future for all.

4 Beliefs and Values

4.1 Environmental Justice and Equity

Environmental justice and equity have been central to Robert F. Kennedy Jr.'s environmental activism and advocacy. Throughout his career, Kennedy has consistently emphasized the importance of ensuring that all communities, regardless of their socioeconomic status or race, have equal access to a clean and healthy environment.

4.1.1 Understanding Environmental Justice

Kennedy's commitment to environmental justice stems from his recognition of the disproportionate impact of pollution and environmental degradation on marginalized communities. He believes that everyone, regardless of their background, deserves to live in a safe and healthy environment. Environmental justice seeks to address the unequal distribution of environmental burdens and benefits, aiming to rectify the historical and ongoing environmental injustices faced by marginalized communities.

4.1.2 Fighting for Marginalized Communities

Kennedy has been a vocal advocate for marginalized communities that bear the brunt of environmental pollution and degradation. He has consistently fought against environmental racism, which refers to the disproportionate exposure of communities of color to environmental hazards. Kennedy believes that these communities have been historically marginalized and neglected, and he strives to amplify their voices and advocate for their rights.

4.1.3 Challenging Environmental Inequities

One of Kennedy's key initiatives in addressing environmental justice is to challenge the systemic inequities that perpetuate environmental harm. He has worked to expose the ways in which corporate interests and government policies often prioritize profit over the well-being of communities. By highlighting these injustices, Kennedy aims to bring about systemic change and create a more equitable and sustainable future.

4.1.4 Advocating for Access to Clean Water

Access to clean water is a fundamental human right, yet many communities, particularly those in low-income areas, lack access to safe drinking water. Kennedy has been at the forefront of advocating for clean water and has worked tirelessly to protect water resources from pollution and contamination. Through his involvement with the Waterkeeper Alliance, he has fought against industrial pollution, agricultural runoff, and other sources of water pollution that disproportionately affect marginalized communities.

4.1.5 Addressing Environmental Health Disparities

Kennedy recognizes the link between environmental health and social justice. He has been a staunch advocate for addressing the health disparities that result from environmental pollution. Many communities living near industrial facilities or toxic waste sites experience higher rates of respiratory illnesses, cancer, and other health issues. Kennedy has worked to raise awareness about these disparities and push for policies that prioritize the health and well-being of all individuals, regardless of their socioeconomic status.

4.1.6 Collaborating with Environmental Justice Organizations

Kennedy understands the importance of collaboration and partnership in advancing environmental justice. He has actively worked with environmental justice organizations and community groups to address the specific needs and concerns of marginalized communities. By amplifying the voices of these communities and supporting their initiatives, Kennedy aims to create a more inclusive and equitable environmental movement.

4.1.7 Promoting Education and Awareness

Education and awareness play a crucial role in achieving environmental justice. Kennedy has been a strong advocate for educating communities about their environmental rights and empowering them to take action. He believes that by providing communities with the knowledge and tools to advocate for themselves, they can effectively challenge environmental injustices and create positive change.

4.1.8 Legislative Efforts for Environmental Justice

Kennedy has also been involved in legislative efforts to promote environmental justice. He has worked to strengthen environmental regulations and push for policies that prioritize the protection of marginalized communities. Kennedy believes that by enacting strong environmental laws and regulations, we can ensure that all communities have equal access to a clean and healthy environment.

In conclusion, Robert F. Kennedy Jr. has been a tireless advocate for environmental justice and equity. His commitment to addressing the disproportionate impact of pollution on marginalized communities has shaped his environmental activism. Through his work, Kennedy has fought for the rights of these communities, challenged systemic inequities, and worked towards creating a more just and sustainable future for all.

4.2 Climate Change and Global Warming

Climate change and global warming have been central issues in Robert F. Kennedy Jr.'s environmental activism. Recognizing the urgent need for action, Kennedy has dedicated much of his career to raising awareness about the devastating effects of climate change and advocating for sustainable solutions. His deep understanding of the science behind climate change and his commitment to environmental justice have made him a prominent voice in the fight against global warming.

4.2.1 Understanding Climate Change

Kennedy's understanding of climate change is rooted in scientific evidence and research. He recognizes that climate change is primarily caused by human activities, particularly the burning of fossil fuels and the release of greenhouse gases into the atmosphere. Kennedy understands that these actions have led to a significant increase in global temperatures, resulting in a wide range of environmental and social impacts.

4.2.2 The Urgency of Action

Kennedy firmly believes that addressing climate change is one of the most pressing challenges of our time. He emphasizes the need for immediate action to mitigate the effects of global warming and prevent further damage to the planet. Kennedy understands that the consequences of inaction are severe, including rising sea levels, extreme weather events, loss of biodiversity, and threats to human health and well-being.

4.2.3 Advocacy for Renewable Energy

One of Kennedy's key strategies for combating climate change is promoting the transition to renewable energy sources. He advocates for the widespread adoption of clean and sustainable energy technologies such as solar, wind, and geothermal power. Kennedy believes that investing in renewable energy not only reduces greenhouse gas emissions but also creates jobs and stimulates economic growth.

4.2.4 Environmental Justice and Climate Change

Kennedy is a strong advocate for environmental justice, recognizing that marginalized communities are disproportionately affected by the impacts of climate change. He highlights the importance of addressing the unequal distribution of environmental burdens and benefits, ensuring that vulnerable populations have access to clean air, water, and a healthy environment. Kennedy believes that climate change solutions must be equitable and inclusive, leaving no one behind.

4.2.5 International Cooperation and Climate Agreements

Kennedy emphasizes the need for international cooperation to effectively address climate change. He supports global efforts such as the Paris Agreement, which aims to limit global warming to well below 2 degrees Celsius above pre-industrial levels. Kennedy believes that international agreements and collaborations are crucial for implementing sustainable policies, sharing knowledge and resources, and achieving meaningful progress in the fight against climate change.

4.2.6 The Role of Corporate Influence

Kennedy is critical of the influence that corporations have on climate change policies and regulations. He argues that powerful industries, particularly those in the fossil fuel sector, often prioritize their own profits over the well-being of the planet and its inhabitants. Kennedy advocates for greater transparency, accountability, and regulation to counteract the undue influence of corporate interests and ensure that environmental decisions are made in the best interest of the public and the planet.

4.2.7 Climate Change Denial and Misinformation

Kennedy has been vocal in debunking climate change denial and misinformation. He recognizes the harmful impact of false narratives that seek to undermine the scientific consensus on climate change. Kennedy emphasizes the importance of evidence-based decision-making and the need to rely on accurate information when formulating climate policies and strategies.

4.2.8 Collaboration and Grassroots Movements

Kennedy believes in the power of collaboration and grassroots movements in addressing climate change. He actively engages with communities, organizations, and individuals working towards sustainable solutions. Kennedy encourages citizen participation, urging people to take action at the local level and hold their elected officials accountable for implementing effective climate policies.

In conclusion, Robert F. Kennedy Jr. is a passionate advocate for addressing climate change and global warming. His understanding of the science, commitment to environmental justice, and emphasis on renewable energy and international cooperation make him a prominent figure in the fight against climate change. Kennedy's efforts to debunk misinformation and corporate influence further contribute to the urgency of taking action. Through collaboration and grassroots movements, he inspires individuals and communities to join the fight for a sustainable and resilient future.

4.3 Corporate Influence on the Environment

Corporate influence on the environment is a significant issue that Robert F. Kennedy Jr. has been vocal about throughout his environmental journey. He firmly believes that corporate interests often prioritize profit over the well-being of the planet and its inhabitants. In this section, we will explore Kennedy's views on corporate influence on the environment and his efforts to combat it.

4.3.1 The Power of Corporations

Kennedy recognizes the immense power that corporations hold in shaping environmental policies and practices. He argues that many corporations prioritize short-term financial gains over long-term sustainability, leading to detrimental effects on the environment. Kennedy believes that corporate influence often leads to the exploitation of natural resources, pollution, and the degradation of ecosystems.

4.3.2 Environmental Regulations and Lobbying

Kennedy has been a staunch advocate for stronger environmental regulations to counterbalance the influence of corporations. He argues that corporations often use their financial resources to lobby against regulations that would hold them accountable for their environmental impact. Kennedy believes that this lobbying power allows corporations to shape legislation in their favor, often at the expense of environmental protection.

4.3.3 Corporate Responsibility and Accountability

One of Kennedy's key beliefs is that corporations should be held accountable for their environmental impact. He argues that companies should take responsibility for the pollution they generate and the resources they consume. Kennedy advocates for corporate transparency, urging companies to disclose their environmental practices and the potential risks they pose to the planet.

4.3.4 Sustainable Business Practices

Kennedy promotes the adoption of sustainable business practices as a way to mitigate the negative impact of corporate activities on the environment. He believes that companies should prioritize renewable energy sources, reduce waste production, and implement eco-friendly manufacturing processes. Kennedy argues that sustainable practices not only benefit the environment but also contribute to long-term economic stability.

4.3.5 Corporate Accountability in the Legal System

Kennedy has been involved in numerous environmental lawsuits against corporations, aiming to hold them accountable for their actions. He believes that legal action is an essential tool in challenging corporate influence and ensuring that companies are held responsible for their environmental harm. Kennedy's involvement in these lawsuits has helped raise awareness about the environmental impact of corporate activities.

4.3.6 Collaboration and Partnerships

Kennedy recognizes the importance of collaboration between environmental organizations and corporations to drive positive change. He believes that by working together, companies and environmental advocates can find innovative solutions to environmental challenges. Kennedy has been involved in partnerships with companies that are committed to sustainable practices, aiming to influence other corporations to follow suit.

4.3.7 Public Awareness and Consumer Choices

Kennedy emphasizes the role of public awareness and consumer choices in influencing corporate behavior. He believes that informed consumers can drive change by supporting companies that prioritize environmental sustainability and boycotting those that do not. Kennedy encourages individuals to educate themselves about the environmental impact of the products they consume and make conscious choices that align with their values.

4.3.8 Political Influence and Campaign Finance Reform

Kennedy acknowledges the influence of corporate campaign contributions on politics and environmental policy. He advocates for campaign finance reform to reduce the influence of corporations on political decision-making. Kennedy believes that by limiting the financial power of corporations in politics, the government can prioritize the interests of the environment and the public.

4.3.9 International Cooperation and Regulation

Kennedy recognizes that corporate influence on the environment is not limited to national boundaries. He emphasizes the need for international cooperation and regulation to address global environmental challenges. Kennedy believes that countries should work together to establish and enforce environmental standards that hold corporations accountable for their actions on a global scale.

In conclusion, Robert F. Kennedy Jr. strongly believes that corporate influence on the environment is a significant obstacle to achieving sustainability. He advocates for stronger regulations, corporate accountability, sustainable business practices, and public awareness to counterbalance the power of corporations. Kennedy's efforts to combat corporate influence have made him a prominent figure in the environmental movement, inspiring others to challenge the status quo and work towards a more sustainable future.

4.4 Public Health and Environmental Impact

Public health and the environment are intricately connected, and Robert F. Kennedy Jr. has been a vocal advocate for recognizing and addressing the impact of environmental issues on human health. Throughout his career, Kennedy has highlighted the importance of understanding the link between environmental degradation and public health, and has worked tirelessly to raise awareness and promote solutions to these pressing challenges.

4.4.1 The Intersection of Public Health and the Environment

Robert F. Kennedy Jr. firmly believes that the health of our planet directly affects the health of its inhabitants. He recognizes that pollution, climate change, and the degradation of natural resources have profound implications for human well-being. Kennedy has been a staunch advocate for understanding and addressing the environmental factors that contribute to a wide range of health issues, including respiratory diseases, cancer, neurological disorders, and developmental problems.

Kennedy's work has focused on highlighting the disproportionate impact of environmental hazards on marginalized communities. He has consistently emphasized the concept of environmental justice, which recognizes that low-income communities and communities of color often bear the brunt of environmental pollution and its associated health risks. By shining a light on these inequities, Kennedy has sought to empower these communities and advocate for policies that promote both environmental sustainability and public health.

4.4.2 Fighting for Clean Water and Air

One of the key areas where Robert F. Kennedy Jr. has made significant contributions is in the fight for clean water and air. As the founder of the

Waterkeeper Alliance, Kennedy has been at the forefront of efforts to protect and restore the world's waterways. He has worked tirelessly to hold polluters accountable and ensure that everyone has access to clean and safe water for drinking, swimming, and fishing.

Kennedy has also been a vocal advocate for clean air, recognizing the detrimental impact of air pollution on public health. He has fought against the expansion of fossil fuel infrastructure and has championed the transition to clean and renewable energy sources. By advocating for stricter regulations and promoting sustainable practices, Kennedy has sought to reduce air pollution and improve the respiratory health of communities across the globe.

4.4.3 Addressing Chemical Exposures and Toxins

Another critical aspect of Robert F. Kennedy Jr.'s work is addressing the impact of chemical exposures and toxins on public health. He has been a leading voice in raising awareness about the dangers of certain chemicals, such as pesticides, lead, and mercury, and their potential to cause serious health problems, particularly in vulnerable populations such as children and pregnant women.

Kennedy has been involved in numerous lawsuits and advocacy campaigns aimed at holding corporations accountable for their role in polluting the environment and exposing communities to harmful chemicals. He has also been a strong proponent of stricter regulations and the development of safer alternatives to toxic substances. By advocating for the reduction of chemical exposures and the promotion of safer alternatives, Kennedy has sought to protect public health and prevent the long-term consequences of chemical pollution.

4.4.4 Promoting a Holistic Approach to Health and the Environment

Robert F. Kennedy Jr. recognizes that addressing public health and environmental issues requires a holistic approach that takes into account the interconnectedness of various factors. He has been a vocal proponent of adopting sustainable practices that not only protect the environment but also promote human health and well-being.

Kennedy has advocated for the promotion of organic farming and the reduction of pesticide use, recognizing the potential health benefits of consuming food that is free from harmful chemicals. He has also championed the importance of access to green spaces and the benefits of spending time in nature for mental and physical health.

Furthermore, Kennedy has been a strong advocate for the integration of environmental education into school curricula. He believes that by educating young people about the importance of environmental stewardship and the impact of environmental issues on public health, we can foster a new generation of informed and engaged citizens who are committed to creating a sustainable and healthy future.

In conclusion, Robert F. Kennedy Jr. has been a tireless advocate for recognizing and addressing the impact of environmental issues on public health. Through his work, he has highlighted the interconnectedness of these two critical areas and has fought for policies and practices that promote both environmental sustainability and human well-being. Kennedy's efforts have not only raised awareness about the importance of protecting our planet but have also inspired individuals and communities to take action and create a healthier and more sustainable future for all.

5 Views on the Murder of His Father

5.1 Assassination of Robert F. Kennedy

The assassination of Robert F. Kennedy on June 5, 1968, was a tragic event that had a profound impact on his family, the nation, and the course of history. Robert F. Kennedy Jr., the third of eleven children born to Robert F. Kennedy and Ethel Skakel Kennedy, was just 14 years old at the time of his father's assassination. This devastating event would shape his life and career in significant ways.

5.1.1 The Tragic Event

On that fateful night, Robert F. Kennedy was at the Ambassador Hotel in Los Angeles, California, celebrating his victory in the California Democratic primary for the presidential nomination. As he exited the hotel's ballroom through the kitchen pantry, he was shot multiple times by Sirhan Sirhan, a 24-year-old Palestinian Arab. The shooting occurred shortly after midnight, and despite immediate medical attention, Robert F. Kennedy succumbed to his injuries the following day.

5.1.2 Investigations and Conspiracy Theories

The assassination of Robert F. Kennedy sparked numerous investigations and conspiracy theories that continue to be debated to this day. The official investigation concluded that Sirhan Sirhan acted alone, motivated by his opposition to Kennedy's support for Israel. However, some individuals and researchers have raised questions about the circumstances surrounding the assassination, suggesting the involvement of additional individuals or groups.

Over the years, various conspiracy theories have emerged, proposing alternative explanations for the events of that night. These theories range from claims of a second gunman to allegations of a larger conspiracy involving government agencies. Despite the persistence of these theories, no conclusive evidence has emerged to support them, and the official account remains the widely accepted explanation.

5.1.3 Impact on Robert F. Kennedy Jr.'s Life and Career

The assassination of his father had a profound impact on Robert F. Kennedy Jr. It not only shaped his worldview but also fueled his passion for justice and advocacy. Growing up without his father, Robert Jr. was inspired by his father's commitment to public service and his dedication to fighting for social and economic justice.

The loss of his father at such a young age instilled in Robert Jr. a deep sense of responsibility to carry on his father's legacy. He became determined to make a difference in the world and to fight for the causes his father held dear. This tragic event served as a catalyst for his environmental activism, as he sought to honor his father's memory by dedicating himself to protecting the planet and its resources.

5.1.4 Advocacy for Justice and Truth

In the aftermath of his father's assassination, Robert F. Kennedy Jr. became an outspoken advocate for justice and truth. He has been a vocal proponent of reopening the investigation into his father's murder, calling for a thorough examination of all available evidence. While acknowledging the pain and grief associated with revisiting such a traumatic event, he believes that a comprehensive and transparent investigation is necessary to uncover the truth and bring closure to the Kennedy family and the American people.

Robert Jr.'s advocacy for justice extends beyond his father's assassination. Throughout his career, he has fought against corruption, corporate influence, and the erosion of democratic values. He has been a staunch advocate for transparency and accountability in government, pushing for greater scrutiny of those in positions of power.

5.1.5 Opposition and Criticism

As a prominent figure in environmental activism and a vocal advocate for justice, Robert F. Kennedy Jr. has faced opposition and criticism from various quarters. Some critics question his motives and accuse him of using his family name for personal gain. Others challenge his views on certain environmental issues, arguing that his positions are extreme or misguided.

Additionally, his advocacy for reopening the investigation into his father's assassination has drawn criticism from those who believe that the case has been thoroughly examined and that further investigation is unnecessary. Some critics argue that revisiting the assassination only serves to perpetuate conspiracy theories and distract from more pressing issues.

Despite the opposition he faces, Robert F. Kennedy Jr. remains steadfast in his beliefs and continues to advocate for justice, environmental protection, and the pursuit of truth.

5.1.6 Presidential Campaign in 2024

In recent years, there has been speculation about Robert F. Kennedy Jr.'s potential run for the presidency in 2024. While he has not officially announced his candidacy, there has been growing support for his potential bid. Many believe that his extensive experience in environmental activism, his commitment to justice, and his family's political legacy make him a compelling candidate.

If he were to run for president, Robert F. Kennedy Jr.'s campaign platform would likely focus on environmental issues, social justice, and the restoration of democratic values. His advocacy for clean energy, protection of natural resources, and sustainable practices would form the foundation of his policy proposals. Additionally, his commitment to fighting corporate influence and promoting transparency in government would be central to his campaign.

However, running for president is not without its challenges and obstacles. Robert F. Kennedy Jr. would face intense scrutiny, both from political opponents and the media. His family's history and the tragic events surrounding his father's assassination would undoubtedly be subjects of public interest and debate. Nevertheless, his potential candidacy has the potential to make a significant impact on the political landscape and inspire a new generation of leaders.

In conclusion, the assassination of Robert F. Kennedy had a profound impact on his son, Robert F. Kennedy Jr. It shaped his worldview, fueled his passion for justice, and inspired his environmental activism. His advocacy for justice and truth, as well as his potential presidential campaign, continue to draw both support and opposition. Despite the challenges he faces, Robert F. Kennedy Jr. remains committed to his beliefs and the pursuit of a better future for all.

5.2 Investigations and Conspiracy Theories

Throughout his life, Robert F. Kennedy Jr. has been confronted with numerous investigations and conspiracy theories surrounding the murder of his father, Robert F. Kennedy. The assassination of his father on June 5, 1968, at the Ambassador Hotel in Los Angeles, California, had a profound impact on Robert Jr.'s life and career. In this section, we will explore the investigations into the assassination and the conspiracy theories that have emerged over the years.

5.2.1 Investigations into the Assassination

Following the tragic event, multiple investigations were conducted to determine the circumstances surrounding the assassination of Robert F. Kennedy. The initial investigation was led by the Los Angeles Police Department (LAPD), which concluded that Sirhan Sirhan, a Palestinian Arab, acted alone in the murder. Sirhan was arrested at the scene and later convicted for the crime.

However, over the years, doubts and questions have arisen regarding the official narrative of the assassination. Some individuals, including Robert F. Kennedy Jr., have called for a reinvestigation into the case, raising concerns about potential inconsistencies and unanswered questions. They believe that there may have been more to the story than what was initially presented.

5.2.2 Conspiracy Theories

Conspiracy theories surrounding the assassination of Robert F. Kennedy have proliferated since the tragic event. These theories propose alternative explanations for the murder, often suggesting the involvement of multiple individuals or organizations. While some of these theories lack substantial evidence, they have gained traction among certain groups and individuals.

One prominent conspiracy theory suggests that there was a larger conspiracy at play, involving multiple gunmen and a cover-up by government agencies. Proponents of this theory argue that Sirhan Sirhan was merely a patsy, used to divert attention from the true culprits. They point to alleged inconsistencies in witness testimonies, the trajectory of the bullets, and the behavior of security personnel as evidence of a broader conspiracy.

Another theory suggests that the Central Intelligence Agency (CIA) or other government agencies were involved in the assassination due to Robert F. Kennedy's political activities and his potential impact on the political landscape. This theory posits that his advocacy for civil rights, opposition to the Vietnam War, and his family's political legacy made him a target for powerful entities seeking to maintain the status quo.

It is important to note that the majority of these conspiracy theories lack credible evidence and have been widely debunked by official investigations and experts. The official investigations, including the LAPD investigation and subsequent inquiries, have not found substantial evidence to support these alternative explanations.

5.2.3 Robert F. Kennedy Jr.'s Perspective

Robert F. Kennedy Jr. has been vocal about his skepticism regarding the official narrative of his father's assassination. He has expressed his belief that there are unanswered questions and inconsistencies that warrant further investigation. Kennedy has called for the release of classified documents related to the case, hoping to shed light on any potential hidden truths.

While Kennedy acknowledges the existence of conspiracy theories, he has been careful not to endorse any specific theory without concrete evidence. Instead, he advocates for a thorough and transparent reinvestigation into the assassination, emphasizing the importance of uncovering the truth for the sake of justice and closure.

5.2.4 Criticism and Opposition

Robert F. Kennedy Jr.'s stance on the assassination of his father has attracted both support and criticism. Some individuals view his calls for reinvestigation as a legitimate pursuit of truth and justice. They appreciate his dedication to uncovering any potential hidden facts surrounding the assassination.

However, there are also those who criticize Kennedy for perpetuating conspiracy theories without sufficient evidence. They argue that his public statements and advocacy for reinvestigation contribute to the proliferation of baseless claims and misinformation. Critics contend that the official investigations have already addressed the key aspects of the case and that further reinvestigation is unnecessary.

It is important to recognize that the assassination of Robert F. Kennedy remains a deeply emotional and sensitive topic for many. The differing perspectives and opinions surrounding the event reflect the complexity of the issue and the ongoing search for truth and closure.

In the face of criticism, Robert F. Kennedy Jr. remains steadfast in his pursuit of justice and truth. He continues to advocate for a reinvestigation into the assassination, emphasizing the importance of transparency and accountability. Kennedy's unwavering commitment to uncovering the truth reflects his deep love and respect for his father's legacy and his desire to ensure that justice is served.

5.3 Impact on Robert F. Kennedy Jr.'s Life and Career

The murder of Robert F. Kennedy, Sr. had a profound impact on the life and career of his son, Robert F. Kennedy Jr. The tragic event not only shaped his personal beliefs and values but also fueled his determination to seek justice and truth. The loss of his father at such a young age left a void in his life, but it also ignited a passion within him to carry on his father's legacy and fight for the causes he believed in.

5.3.1 Shaping Personal Beliefs and Values

The assassination of his father deeply influenced Robert F. Kennedy Jr.'s worldview and instilled in him a strong sense of social justice. Witnessing the impact of his father's work and the injustices he fought against, Kennedy developed a deep commitment to fighting for the rights of the marginalized and the protection of the environment. He saw firsthand the power of using his voice and platform to advocate for those who couldn't speak for themselves.

5.3.2 Continuing the Kennedy Legacy

Robert F. Kennedy Jr. was determined to carry on the legacy of his family, which was rooted in public service and activism. He recognized the responsibility he had to make a positive impact on the world, just as his father and uncles had done before him. Kennedy understood that he had a unique opportunity to use his name and influence to effect change and fight for causes he believed in, particularly in the realm of environmental activism.

5.3.3 Environmental Activism as a Path

The murder of his father propelled Robert F. Kennedy Jr. towards a career in environmental activism. He recognized the interconnectedness of social justice and environmental issues, understanding that marginalized communities often bear the brunt of environmental degradation. Kennedy's commitment to

environmental causes became a central focus of his life and career, as he
sought to protect natural resources, advocate for clean energy initiatives, and
promote sustainable practices.

5.3.4 Seeking Justice and Truth

The murder of Robert F. Kennedy Sr. sparked a lifelong quest for justice and
truth in his son. Over the years, Robert F. Kennedy Jr. has tirelessly
investigated the circumstances surrounding his father's assassination, delving
into conspiracy theories and challenging the official narrative. His pursuit of
the truth has not only been a personal journey but also a way to honor his
father's memory and ensure that justice is served.

5.3.5 Advocacy and Opposition

Robert F. Kennedy Jr.'s outspoken views on the murder of his father have
garnered both support and opposition. While many admire his dedication to
seeking justice and his relentless pursuit of the truth, others have criticized him
for perpetuating conspiracy theories. Kennedy's advocacy for justice and truth
has faced challenges and opposition from those who prefer to accept the
official narrative and discourage further investigation.

5.3.6 Impact on Career and Activism

The impact of his father's murder on Robert F. Kennedy Jr.'s life and career
cannot be overstated. It served as a catalyst for his environmental activism and
shaped his commitment to fighting for justice. Kennedy's relentless pursuit of
truth and justice has not only influenced his personal life but also his
professional endeavors. His advocacy work, lawsuits, and environmental
initiatives have made a significant impact on the environmental movement and
have inspired others to take action.

5.3.7 Presidential Campaign in 2024

The impact of his father's murder also played a role in Robert F. Kennedy Jr.'s decision to run for president in 2024. He saw the opportunity to use his platform to address the issues he cared deeply about, including environmental justice, corporate influence, and public health. Kennedy's campaign aimed to bring attention to these critical issues and offer solutions that aligned with his beliefs and values. While his campaign faced challenges and obstacles, his run for president had a significant impact on the political landscape, sparking conversations and debates about the pressing issues facing our society.

In conclusion, the murder of Robert F. Kennedy Sr. had a profound impact on the life and career of his son, Robert F. Kennedy Jr. It shaped his personal beliefs and values, fueled his commitment to seeking justice and truth, and propelled him towards a career in environmental activism. Kennedy's advocacy work and his run for president in 2024 have made a lasting impact on the environmental movement and the political landscape. Despite facing opposition and challenges, he continues to inspire others and carry on the Kennedy legacy of public service and activism.

5.4 Advocacy for Justice and Truth

Robert F. Kennedy Jr. has been a staunch advocate for justice and truth throughout his life and career. His unwavering commitment to seeking justice and uncovering the truth has been evident in his work as an environmental activist, as well as in his pursuit of answers surrounding the murder of his father, Robert F. Kennedy.

5.4.1 Seeking Justice for His Father

The assassination of Robert F. Kennedy in 1968 was a devastating event that had a profound impact on his family, particularly on Robert F. Kennedy Jr. As he grew older, he became increasingly determined to uncover the truth behind his father's murder. Kennedy Jr. has been vocal in his belief that there were deeper forces at play and that the official explanation of the assassination does not tell the whole story.

Kennedy Jr. has tirelessly advocated for a thorough investigation into his father's assassination, pushing for the release of classified documents and challenging the official narrative. He has called for transparency and accountability, believing that the truth about his father's murder has been obscured for far too long. His advocacy for justice in this matter has been driven by a deep desire to honor his father's memory and ensure that the truth is known.

5.4.2 Challenging Conspiracy Theories

Over the years, there have been numerous conspiracy theories surrounding the assassination of Robert F. Kennedy. Some of these theories suggest that there was a larger conspiracy involved, while others question the official account of the events. Kennedy Jr. has been vocal in his skepticism of the official explanation and has actively engaged with various theories and investigations.

However, it is important to note that Kennedy Jr. has also been critical of unfounded and baseless conspiracy theories. He has emphasized the importance of evidence-based research and has called for responsible and credible investigations into his father's assassination. Kennedy Jr. has consistently sought to separate fact from fiction and has been a strong advocate for the pursuit of truth through rigorous investigation.

5.4.3 Advocacy for Justice in Other Areas

Beyond his personal quest for justice in his father's case, Robert F. Kennedy Jr. has been a tireless advocate for justice in various other areas. He has used his platform and influence to shed light on issues such as environmental justice, corporate accountability, and public health.

Kennedy Jr. has been a vocal critic of corporate influence on the environment and has fought against the undue influence of powerful industries on environmental policy. He has advocated for the rights of marginalized communities who often bear the brunt of environmental degradation and has called for equitable solutions that prioritize the well-being of all.

Additionally, Kennedy Jr. has been a strong advocate for public health, particularly in relation to the impact of environmental factors on human well-being. He has raised awareness about the dangers of toxic chemicals and pollutants, and has worked to hold polluting industries accountable for their actions. His advocacy for justice extends beyond his personal experiences and encompasses a broader commitment to creating a more just and equitable society.

5.4.4 Facing Opposition and Criticism

As a prominent figure in the environmental movement and a vocal advocate for justice, Robert F. Kennedy Jr. has faced his fair share of opposition and criticism. His outspoken views and willingness to challenge powerful interests have made him a target for those who disagree with his positions.

Critics of Kennedy Jr. often accuse him of being a conspiracy theorist or of spreading misinformation. However, it is important to note that Kennedy Jr. has consistently emphasized the importance of evidence-based research and has called for responsible and credible investigations. He has been transparent about his sources and has sought to separate fact from fiction.

Despite the opposition he faces, Kennedy Jr. remains steadfast in his commitment to justice and truth. He continues to advocate for transparency, accountability, and the pursuit of truth in all areas of his work. His unwavering dedication to these principles has earned him respect and admiration from many who share his commitment to justice and truth.

5.4.5 Presidential Campaign in 2024

In recent years, there has been speculation about Robert F. Kennedy Jr.'s potential run for the presidency in 2024. While he has not officially announced his candidacy, Kennedy Jr. has expressed his motivations and considerations for a potential presidential campaign.

If he were to run for president, Kennedy Jr. has stated that his campaign would be centered around issues of environmental justice, public health, and corporate accountability. He believes that these issues are of utmost importance and require urgent attention at the highest levels of government.

Kennedy Jr. acknowledges the challenges and obstacles that come with running for president, but he remains optimistic about the potential impact his campaign could have on the political landscape. He sees his potential candidacy as an opportunity to bring these critical issues to the forefront of national discourse and to inspire meaningful change.

In conclusion, Robert F. Kennedy Jr.'s advocacy for justice and truth is a defining aspect of his life and career. From seeking justice for his father's assassination to challenging conspiracy theories and advocating for justice in various areas, Kennedy Jr. has consistently demonstrated his commitment to uncovering the truth and fighting for a more just and equitable society. Despite facing opposition and criticism, he remains steadfast in his pursuit of justice and truth, and his potential presidential campaign in 2024 could further amplify his advocacy on a national scale.

6 Opposition and Controversies

6.1 Critics of Robert F. Kennedy Jr.

As a prominent environmental activist and advocate, Robert F. Kennedy
Jr. has faced his fair share of criticism and opposition. While his work has
garnered widespread support and admiration, there are those who challenge his
views, question his methods, and even dispute his credibility. This section will
explore some of the criticisms that have been directed towards Kennedy
Jr. throughout his career.

6.1.1 Skepticism of Vaccination Stance

One of the most significant areas of contention surrounding Robert F.
Kennedy Jr. is his stance on vaccinations. Kennedy Jr. has been a vocal critic
of certain vaccine practices, particularly those involving the use of mercury-
based preservatives. He has raised concerns about potential links between
vaccines and certain health conditions, such as autism. However, his views on
this topic have been widely criticized by the scientific community, which
overwhelmingly supports the safety and efficacy of vaccines. Many experts
argue that Kennedy Jr.'s claims are not supported by rigorous scientific
evidence and that his advocacy against vaccines poses a risk to public health.

6.1.2 Opposition from the Fossil Fuel Industry

Given his strong advocacy for clean energy and environmental protection, it is
no surprise that Robert F. Kennedy Jr. has faced opposition from the fossil fuel
industry. His efforts to promote renewable energy sources and challenge the
influence of oil and gas companies have made him a target for criticism.
Critics argue that Kennedy Jr.'s positions on energy policy are unrealistic and
economically unfeasible. They claim that his emphasis on transitioning away
from fossil fuels disregards the economic impact on industries and
communities that rely on these resources. Additionally, some opponents
accuse Kennedy Jr. of being overly idealistic and failing to consider the
practical challenges of implementing his proposed solutions.

6.1.3 Accusations of Misinformation and Conspiracy Theories

Kennedy Jr.'s outspoken nature and willingness to challenge established institutions have led to accusations of spreading misinformation and endorsing conspiracy theories. Some critics argue that his views on certain environmental issues, such as climate change and the safety of genetically modified organisms (GMOs), are not grounded in scientific consensus. They claim that Kennedy Jr. selectively presents information to support his arguments while disregarding opposing evidence. Additionally, his association with individuals and groups that promote conspiracy theories, such as those questioning the safety of vaccines, has further fueled skepticism and criticism.

6.1.4 Political Bias and Partisanship

As a member of the Kennedy family, Robert F. Kennedy Jr. has often been accused of leveraging his name and connections for political gain. Critics argue that his environmental activism is driven by a partisan agenda rather than a genuine commitment to the cause. They claim that Kennedy Jr. uses his platform to advance the interests of the Democratic Party and promote policies that align with his political affiliations. This perception of bias has led some to question the objectivity and credibility of his work.

6.1.5 Personal Attacks and Character Assassination

Unfortunately, the realm of public discourse is not immune to personal attacks and character assassination, and Robert F. Kennedy Jr. has not been exempt from such treatment. Critics have targeted his personal life, including his past struggles with addiction and his divorce, as a means to discredit him and undermine his credibility. These attacks often serve as distractions from the substantive issues at hand and attempt to tarnish Kennedy Jr.'s reputation.

While critics of Robert F. Kennedy Jr. raise valid concerns and engage in legitimate debates, it is important to recognize that opposition is an inherent part of any public figure's journey. Kennedy Jr.'s work and beliefs have undoubtedly sparked controversy and disagreement, but they have also inspired meaningful discussions and positive change. It is through open dialogue and respectful engagement that progress can be made in addressing the complex environmental challenges we face as a society.

6.2 Challenges and Opposition to Environmental Activism

Robert F. Kennedy Jr.'s environmental activism has not been without its challenges and opposition. As a prominent figure in the field, he has faced criticism and resistance from various sources. This section will explore some of the key challenges and opposition that Kennedy has encountered throughout his environmental journey.

6.2.1 Industry Interests and Lobbying

One of the primary challenges faced by environmental activists like Robert F. Kennedy Jr. is the opposition from powerful industry interests. The fossil fuel industry, for example, has a significant influence on policy-making and has often opposed environmental regulations that could impact their profits. Kennedy's advocacy for clean energy and sustainable practices has put him at odds with these influential entities.

The lobbying power of these industries has often resulted in the dilution or rejection of environmental legislation. They have also funded campaigns to discredit environmental activists and their work. Kennedy's efforts to promote renewable energy and reduce reliance on fossil fuels have faced significant opposition from these vested interests.

6.2.2 Political Resistance

Environmental activism is inherently political, and it often faces resistance from politicians who prioritize short-term economic gains over long-term environmental sustainability. Kennedy's advocacy for stronger environmental regulations and policies has been met with opposition from politicians who are influenced by industry interests or who prioritize other issues over environmental concerns.

Kennedy's work with the Waterkeeper Alliance and his involvement in environmental lawsuits have sometimes put him at odds with government agencies and officials. This has led to legal battles and bureaucratic hurdles that have hindered progress in addressing environmental issues.

6.2.3 Disinformation and Attacks

Opponents of environmental activism have also resorted to disinformation campaigns and personal attacks to undermine the credibility of activists like Kennedy. False narratives and misinformation about the environmental movement and its goals have been spread to create doubt and confusion among the public.

Kennedy has been the target of such attacks, with critics questioning his motives and spreading baseless accusations. These attacks aim to discredit his work and undermine the legitimacy of the environmental movement as a whole. However, Kennedy has consistently refuted these claims and has remained steadfast in his commitment to environmental causes.

6.2.4 Polarization and Public Perception

Environmental issues have become increasingly polarized in recent years, with debates often framed as a conflict between economic growth and environmental protection. This polarization has created challenges for environmental activists like Kennedy, as they face resistance from those who view their efforts as a threat to their livelihoods or personal freedoms.

Kennedy's outspoken views and his involvement in high-profile lawsuits have made him a polarizing figure. Some perceive him as an environmental champion, while others view him as an obstructionist or an extremist. This polarization has made it difficult to have constructive dialogues and find common ground on environmental issues.

6.2.5 Legal and Regulatory Challenges

The legal and regulatory landscape surrounding environmental issues can be complex and challenging. Environmental activists often face obstacles in navigating these systems and bringing about meaningful change. Kennedy's work with the Waterkeeper Alliance and his involvement in environmental lawsuits have required significant resources and expertise to overcome legal hurdles.

Opponents of environmental activism have also used legal means to challenge and delay environmental initiatives. This has resulted in lengthy legal battles and delays in implementing necessary environmental regulations. Kennedy's commitment to fighting for environmental justice has required him to navigate these challenges and find innovative ways to overcome legal and regulatory obstacles.

Despite these challenges and opposition, Robert F. Kennedy Jr. has remained steadfast in his commitment to environmental activism. His resilience and determination have allowed him to continue advocating for sustainable practices, clean energy initiatives, and the protection of natural resources. Kennedy's ability to navigate these obstacles and maintain his focus on the greater good is a testament to his dedication and passion for the environment.

6.3 Debunking Misinformation and Attacks

In the world of environmental activism, Robert F. Kennedy Jr. has faced his fair share of opposition and controversy. As a prominent figure in the movement, he has been subjected to misinformation and attacks from various sources. However, it is important to separate fact from fiction and debunk the falsehoods that have been spread about him.

6.3.1 False Accusations and Conspiracy Theories

Throughout his career, Robert F. Kennedy Jr. has been the target of false accusations and conspiracy theories. One of the most persistent and baseless claims is that he is an anti-vaccine advocate. This misinformation stems from his advocacy for vaccine safety and his concern about the potential risks associated with certain vaccines. However, Kennedy has consistently clarified that he is not against vaccines but rather supports rigorous safety testing and transparency in the vaccine industry.

Another unfounded accusation is that Kennedy is a proponent of 5G conspiracy theories. This claim suggests that he believes 5G technology is harmful to human health and the environment. In reality, Kennedy has expressed concerns about the potential health effects of electromagnetic radiation and has called for further research to ensure the safety of 5G technology. However, he has not endorsed any conspiracy theories related to 5G.

6.3.2 Attacks on Character and Motives

As a prominent environmental activist, Robert F. Kennedy Jr. has faced personal attacks on his character and motives. Critics have attempted to discredit him by questioning his integrity and suggesting that his environmental advocacy is driven by personal gain or political motives. These attacks are often unfounded and fail to acknowledge Kennedy's long-standing commitment to environmental causes.

Kennedy's dedication to environmental protection can be traced back to his childhood and upbringing. Growing up in a family that valued public service and social justice, he developed a deep sense of responsibility to protect the natural world. His advocacy work and involvement in organizations such as the Waterkeeper Alliance demonstrate his genuine commitment to preserving the environment for future generations.

6.3.3 Fact-Checking and Evidence-Based Advocacy

In the face of misinformation and attacks, Robert F. Kennedy Jr. has consistently relied on fact-checking and evidence-based advocacy. He has emphasized the importance of scientific research and data-driven decision-making in addressing environmental issues. Kennedy's approach is grounded in a deep understanding of the complexities of environmental challenges and the need for informed solutions.

Kennedy's advocacy work has been supported by a wealth of scientific evidence and expert opinions. He has collaborated with renowned scientists, environmentalists, and legal experts to build strong cases for environmental protection. His efforts have resulted in significant victories, such as the successful lawsuits against polluters and the establishment of environmental policies and regulations.

6.3.4 Engaging in Constructive Dialogue

Despite facing opposition and controversy, Robert F. Kennedy Jr. has consistently engaged in constructive dialogue with his critics. He has welcomed open discussions and debates on environmental issues, recognizing the importance of diverse perspectives in finding effective solutions. Kennedy's willingness to engage with those who disagree with him demonstrates his commitment to fostering understanding and finding common ground.

Kennedy has also been proactive in addressing misconceptions and clarifying his positions. Through interviews, speeches, and public appearances, he has taken the opportunity to provide accurate information and dispel false narratives. By engaging in open and honest conversations, Kennedy has sought to bridge the gap between differing viewpoints and promote informed decision-making.

6.3.5 Upholding the Green Legacy

In the face of misinformation and attacks, Robert F. Kennedy Jr. remains steadfast in his commitment to environmental activism. He continues to advocate for the protection of natural resources, the promotion of sustainable practices, and the pursuit of environmental justice. Kennedy's unwavering dedication to these causes is a testament to his resilience and determination to leave a positive impact on the world.

As individuals, it is crucial to critically evaluate the information we encounter and seek out reliable sources. By debunking misinformation and understanding the true accomplishments and beliefs of Robert F. Kennedy Jr., we can appreciate the significant contributions he has made to the environmental movement.

6.4 Navigating Controversies and Public Perception

Navigating controversies and managing public perception is an inevitable challenge for any public figure, and Robert F. Kennedy Jr. is no exception. Throughout his environmental journey, Kennedy has faced opposition and criticism from various quarters. This section explores some of the controversies surrounding him and how he has managed public perception.

6.4.1 Addressing Criticism and Opposition

As a prominent environmental activist, Kennedy has not been immune to criticism. Some critics argue that his privileged background and family name have given him undue influence and access to resources. Others question his qualifications and expertise in environmental issues. However, Kennedy has consistently addressed these criticisms by emphasizing his commitment to the cause and his extensive experience in the field.

Kennedy has always been open to constructive dialogue and has engaged with his critics to address their concerns. He has actively participated in debates and discussions, providing evidence-based arguments to support his positions. By engaging with his opponents, Kennedy has demonstrated his willingness to listen and learn from different perspectives, further enhancing his credibility as an environmental advocate.

6.4.2 Handling Misinformation and Attacks

In the age of social media and online platforms, misinformation and personal attacks have become common tactics used against public figures. Kennedy has been a target of such attacks, with false information and conspiracy theories being spread about him. However, he has consistently taken a proactive approach to debunking misinformation and setting the record straight.

Kennedy has utilized various platforms, including interviews, speeches, and social media, to address false claims and provide accurate information. He has relied on scientific evidence and expert opinions to counter misinformation, ensuring that the public has access to reliable information. By doing so, Kennedy has demonstrated his commitment to transparency and truth, even in the face of adversity.

6.4.3 Building Trust and Credibility

Public perception plays a crucial role in the success of any advocacy campaign. Kennedy understands the importance of building trust and credibility with the public. Throughout his environmental journey, he has consistently demonstrated his dedication to the cause and his unwavering commitment to protecting the environment.

Kennedy's extensive experience and knowledge in environmental issues have contributed to his credibility as an advocate. He has worked tirelessly to promote sustainable practices, protect natural resources, and advocate for clean energy initiatives. By leading by example and actively engaging with communities, Kennedy has gained the trust and respect of many individuals and organizations.

6.4.4 Balancing Personal and Professional Life

Being in the public eye can take a toll on personal life, and Kennedy has had to navigate the challenges of balancing his personal and professional commitments. As a father and husband, he has strived to maintain a healthy work-life balance, ensuring that he is present for his family while pursuing his environmental activism.

Kennedy's ability to prioritize and manage his time effectively has allowed him to fulfill his responsibilities both personally and professionally. He has emphasized the importance of self-care and taking time for oneself, recognizing that maintaining personal well-being is essential for long-term success in any endeavor.

6.4.5 Public Perception and the 2024 Presidential Campaign

As Kennedy contemplates a run for the presidency in 2024, public perception will undoubtedly play a significant role in shaping his campaign. While he has a strong base of supporters who admire his environmental advocacy, he will also face scrutiny and opposition from those who disagree with his views.

To navigate the complexities of a presidential campaign, Kennedy will need to effectively communicate his policy proposals, address concerns raised by opponents, and build a broad coalition of supporters. By emphasizing his track record of environmental accomplishments and his commitment to justice and equity, Kennedy can appeal to a wide range of voters who prioritize these issues.

Ultimately, the success of Kennedy's campaign will depend on his ability to connect with voters, address their concerns, and inspire them with his vision for a sustainable and just future. By staying true to his values and effectively managing controversies and public perception, Kennedy can make a lasting impact on the political landscape and continue his environmental legacy.

7 Presidential Campaign in 2024

7.1 Motivations and Decision to Run

Robert F. Kennedy Jr.'s decision to run for President in 2024 was motivated by a deep sense of duty and a desire to continue his lifelong commitment to environmental activism and social justice. Throughout his career, Kennedy had witnessed firsthand the devastating impact of environmental degradation and corporate influence on communities and individuals. He believed that the time had come for a leader who would prioritize the health of the planet and its people over profit and power.

Kennedy's motivations to run for President were rooted in his unwavering belief in the power of government to effect positive change. He saw the presidency as a platform to amplify his voice and advocate for policies that would protect the environment, promote clean energy, and ensure social and economic justice for all Americans. Kennedy recognized that the challenges facing the nation and the world required bold and decisive action, and he believed that he was uniquely positioned to lead that charge.

One of the key factors that influenced Kennedy's decision to run was his family legacy. As a member of the Kennedy family, he was acutely aware of the impact that his relatives had made on American politics and society. The Kennedy family had a long history of public service and a commitment to fighting for the rights of the marginalized and disadvantaged. Kennedy felt a deep sense of responsibility to carry on this legacy and continue the work that his father, Robert F. Kennedy, and his uncle, President John F. Kennedy, had started.

Kennedy's outspoken views on the murder of his father also played a significant role in his decision to run for President. The assassination of Robert F. Kennedy in 1968 had a profound impact on his son's life and shaped his worldview. Kennedy believed that his father's murder was not simply the act of a lone gunman, but rather part of a larger conspiracy. He dedicated much of his life to investigating the circumstances surrounding his father's death and seeking justice for him. Running for President provided Kennedy with a platform to bring attention to his father's case and advocate for truth and accountability.

Kennedy was well aware that his decision to run for President would not be without challenges and opposition. Throughout his career as an environmental activist, he had faced criticism and pushback from those who disagreed with his views and his advocacy. Some critics accused him of being an "environmental extremist" or a "radical" due to his strong stance on issues such as climate change and corporate accountability. However, Kennedy remained steadfast in his convictions and saw these challenges as opportunities to educate and engage in meaningful dialogue.

In terms of his campaign platform and policy proposals, Kennedy focused on a comprehensive approach to addressing the pressing issues facing the nation. His platform included ambitious goals for transitioning to a clean energy economy, protecting natural resources, and promoting sustainable practices. He advocated for stronger environmental regulations, increased investment in renewable energy, and the creation of green jobs. Kennedy also emphasized the need for environmental justice and equity, recognizing that marginalized communities are disproportionately affected by pollution and environmental hazards.

Kennedy's decision to run for President in 2024 had a significant impact on the political landscape. His candidacy energized and mobilized a diverse coalition of supporters who shared his vision for a more sustainable and just future. Kennedy's campaign brought environmental issues to the forefront of the national conversation and forced other candidates to address these critical concerns. While he faced formidable obstacles and ultimately did not secure the nomination, his campaign left a lasting impact on the political discourse and inspired a new generation of activists and leaders.

In conclusion, Robert F. Kennedy Jr.'s motivations to run for President in 2024 were driven by a deep sense of duty, a desire to continue his environmental activism, and a commitment to social justice. His decision was influenced by his family legacy, his outspoken views on his father's murder, and his belief in the power of government to effect positive change. Despite facing opposition and challenges, Kennedy's campaign had a significant impact on the political landscape and inspired a new generation of leaders to prioritize the environment and social justice in their own pursuits.

7.2 Campaign Platform and Policy Proposals

As Robert F. Kennedy Jr. embarks on his presidential campaign in 2024, he brings with him a comprehensive platform and a set of policy proposals that reflect his lifelong dedication to environmental activism and social justice. Kennedy's campaign is centered around addressing the urgent challenges facing our planet and ensuring a sustainable and equitable future for all. Here, we will explore his campaign platform and the policy proposals he has put forth.

7.2.1 Environmental Policy and Climate Change

At the core of Kennedy's campaign platform is his commitment to combating climate change and protecting the environment. He advocates for the implementation of bold and comprehensive environmental policies that prioritize the transition to clean and renewable energy sources. Kennedy proposes investing in research and development of sustainable technologies, promoting energy efficiency, and supporting the expansion of renewable energy infrastructure.

Kennedy also emphasizes the importance of international cooperation in addressing climate change. He proposes rejoining the Paris Agreement and strengthening global efforts to reduce greenhouse gas emissions. Additionally, he advocates for the establishment of international agreements to protect vulnerable ecosystems and biodiversity.

7.2.2 Environmental Justice and Equity

Recognizing the disproportionate impact of environmental degradation on marginalized communities, Kennedy places a strong emphasis on environmental justice and equity in his campaign platform. He proposes implementing policies that address the unequal distribution of environmental burdens and benefits. This includes ensuring access to clean air, water, and healthy food for all communities, regardless of their socioeconomic status.

Kennedy also advocates for the inclusion of marginalized communities in decision-making processes related to environmental policies. He believes that their voices should be heard and their concerns should be addressed to create a more just and sustainable society.

7.2.3 Public Health and Environmental Impact

Understanding the interconnectedness of environmental issues and public health, Kennedy's campaign platform prioritizes the protection of public health from environmental hazards. He proposes strengthening regulations on toxic substances, reducing exposure to harmful pollutants, and promoting the use of safe and sustainable products.

Kennedy also advocates for increased funding for research on the health impacts of environmental factors, such as air and water pollution, climate change, and exposure to hazardous chemicals. He believes that by addressing these issues, we can improve public health outcomes and create a healthier future for all.

7.2.4 Conservation and Protection of Natural Resources

As an avid conservationist, Kennedy's campaign platform includes policies aimed at preserving and protecting our natural resources. He proposes expanding protected areas, national parks, and wildlife sanctuaries to safeguard biodiversity and promote ecological balance.

Kennedy also advocates for sustainable land and water management practices, including the restoration of degraded ecosystems and the protection of critical habitats. He believes that by conserving our natural resources, we can ensure their availability for future generations and maintain the delicate balance of our planet's ecosystems.

7.2.5 Sustainable Agriculture and Food Systems

Recognizing the importance of sustainable agriculture in addressing environmental and food security challenges, Kennedy's campaign platform includes proposals to promote regenerative farming practices, reduce pesticide use, and support local and organic food production. He believes in the importance of transitioning towards a more sustainable and resilient food system that prioritizes the health of both people and the planet.

Kennedy also advocates for policies that promote food justice and access to healthy and affordable food for all communities. He supports initiatives that address food deserts, promote urban farming, and ensure fair wages and working conditions for agricultural workers.

7.2.6 Renewable Energy and Infrastructure

In line with his commitment to clean energy, Kennedy's campaign platform includes proposals to invest in renewable energy infrastructure and accelerate the transition to a carbon-neutral economy. He advocates for the expansion of solar and wind energy projects, the development of energy storage technologies, and the electrification of transportation.

Kennedy also emphasizes the importance of investing in sustainable and resilient infrastructure to mitigate the impacts of climate change. He proposes the modernization of the nation's infrastructure to withstand extreme weather events and the integration of climate resilience into urban planning and development.

7.2.7 Education and Awareness

Recognizing the need for widespread education and awareness on environmental issues, Kennedy's campaign platform includes proposals to integrate environmental education into school curricula at all levels. He believes that by fostering environmental literacy, we can empower future generations to become stewards of the planet.

Kennedy also advocates for public awareness campaigns and initiatives that promote sustainable practices and encourage individuals, businesses, and communities to take action in reducing their environmental footprint.

In conclusion, Robert F. Kennedy Jr.'s campaign platform and policy proposals reflect his deep commitment to environmental activism, social justice, and the well-being of future generations. Through his comprehensive platform, he aims to address the urgent challenges of climate change, promote environmental justice, protect public health, conserve natural resources, and build a sustainable and equitable future for all.

7.3 Challenges and Obstacles

Running for president in 2024 presents Robert F. Kennedy Jr. with numerous challenges and obstacles. While he has a strong track record as an environmental activist and has made significant contributions to the field, entering the political arena on a national scale brings its own set of difficulties. In this section, we will explore some of the challenges and obstacles that Kennedy faces as he embarks on his presidential campaign.

7.3.1 Political Establishment Resistance

One of the primary challenges Kennedy faces is resistance from the political establishment. As a member of the Kennedy family, he carries the weight of their legacy, which can both work in his favor and against him. While the Kennedy name is synonymous with political influence and progressive values, it also attracts scrutiny and skepticism from those who view him as a product of privilege. This resistance from the political establishment can manifest in various ways, including opposition from party insiders, lack of endorsements, and limited access to fundraising networks.

7.3.2 Public Perception and Media Scrutiny

Running for president means being under constant public scrutiny. Kennedy's every move, statement, and action will be analyzed and dissected by the media and the public. As a prominent figure in the environmental movement, he has already faced criticism and controversy, which may be amplified during his campaign. The media's portrayal of Kennedy can significantly impact public perception and ultimately influence his chances of success. It is crucial for him to navigate this landscape carefully, ensuring that his message and intentions are accurately conveyed to the public.

7.3.3 Opposition from Special Interest Groups

Kennedy's strong stance against corporate influence on the environment and his advocacy for environmental justice may face opposition from powerful special interest groups. These groups often have significant financial resources and political influence, which they can use to undermine Kennedy's campaign. Their opposition may come in the form of negative advertising, lobbying efforts, or attempts to discredit his environmental credentials. Overcoming this opposition will require Kennedy to rally grassroots support and build a broad coalition of like-minded individuals and organizations.

7.3.4 Balancing Environmental Priorities with Broader Policy Issues

While Kennedy's environmental activism is at the core of his campaign, he must also address a wide range of policy issues that are of concern to the American people. Balancing his environmental priorities with broader policy issues such as healthcare, education, and the economy can be challenging. Kennedy will need to articulate a comprehensive vision that demonstrates how his environmental agenda aligns with the broader needs and aspirations of the country. Failure to strike this balance may limit his appeal to a broader electorate.

7.3.5 Overcoming Partisan Divisions

In today's highly polarized political climate, overcoming partisan divisions is a significant challenge for any candidate. Kennedy's campaign will need to appeal to voters across the political spectrum, including Democrats, Republicans, and independents. While his environmental advocacy may resonate strongly with progressive voters, he will need to find common ground with conservatives and moderates to build a broad-based coalition. This requires effective communication, a focus on shared values, and a willingness to engage in constructive dialogue with individuals who may hold differing views.

7.3.6 Fundraising and Financial Resources

Running a successful presidential campaign requires substantial financial resources. Kennedy will need to raise significant funds to support his campaign infrastructure, staff, travel, advertising, and other essential expenses. While his family's name and network may provide some advantages, he will still need to compete with other well-funded candidates. Building a robust fundraising operation and attracting grassroots support will be critical to his campaign's success.

7.3.7 Managing Personal and Professional Life

Running for president is an all-consuming endeavor that demands immense time and energy. Kennedy will need to navigate the challenges of managing his personal and professional life while on the campaign trail. Balancing his responsibilities as an environmental advocate, a family man, and a candidate can be demanding and may require making difficult choices. Maintaining a healthy work-life balance and ensuring personal well-being will be essential for his long-term success.

In conclusion, Robert F. Kennedy Jr. faces numerous challenges and obstacles as he embarks on his presidential campaign in 2024. These challenges include resistance from the political establishment, public perception and media scrutiny, opposition from special interest groups, balancing environmental priorities with broader policy issues, overcoming partisan divisions, fundraising, and managing personal and professional life. Successfully navigating these challenges will require strategic planning, effective communication, and building a broad-based coalition of supporters who share his vision for a sustainable and just future.

7.4 Impact on the Political Landscape

Robert F. Kennedy Jr.'s decision to run for President in 2024 had a significant impact on the political landscape of the United States. As a prominent environmental activist and lawyer, Kennedy brought a unique perspective and set of policy proposals to the table. His campaign not only focused on environmental issues but also addressed broader social and economic challenges facing the nation.

7.4.1 Shifting the Political Discourse

Kennedy's presidential campaign played a crucial role in shifting the political discourse towards environmental sustainability and social justice. By placing these issues at the forefront of his platform, he forced other candidates and political parties to address them more seriously. Kennedy's campaign brought attention to the urgent need for action on climate change, the protection of natural resources, and the promotion of sustainable practices.

7.4.2 Energizing the Environmental Movement

Kennedy's candidacy energized the environmental movement and mobilized a new generation of activists. His long-standing commitment to environmental causes and his ability to communicate complex issues in a relatable manner resonated with many voters. Kennedy's campaign rallies and events became platforms for raising awareness about environmental challenges and inspiring individuals to take action in their own communities.

7.4.3 Expanding the Democratic Party's Agenda

Kennedy's campaign pushed the Democratic Party to expand its agenda and prioritize environmental issues. His policy proposals, such as transitioning to clean energy, investing in green infrastructure, and addressing environmental justice, influenced the party's platform and policy discussions. Kennedy's candidacy challenged the party to take bolder steps towards addressing climate change and promoting sustainable development.

7.4.4 Engaging New Constituencies

Kennedy's campaign attracted support from a diverse range of constituencies, including environmentalists, social justice advocates, and young voters. His ability to connect environmental issues with broader concerns, such as public health, economic inequality, and racial justice, resonated with these groups. Kennedy's campaign brought new voices into the political process and expanded the coalition of supporters advocating for progressive environmental policies.

7.4.5 Challenging the Status Quo

Kennedy's run for President challenged the status quo and the influence of corporate interests in politics. His outspoken criticism of corporate influence on the environment and his calls for stricter regulations on polluting industries resonated with many Americans who felt that their voices were being ignored. Kennedy's campaign highlighted the need for campaign finance reform and greater transparency in political decision-making.

7.4.6 Inspiring Future Leaders

Kennedy's presidential campaign inspired a new generation of leaders who are passionate about environmental issues and social justice. His commitment to public service and his ability to mobilize grassroots support served as a model for aspiring activists and politicians. Kennedy's campaign showed that it is possible to make a difference and effect change through political engagement and advocacy.

7.4.7 Shaping the Democratic Party's Future

Kennedy's candidacy had a lasting impact on the future direction of the Democratic Party. His emphasis on environmental sustainability, social justice, and corporate accountability influenced the party's policy agenda and platform. Kennedy's campaign helped shape the party's approach to addressing climate change and promoting a more equitable and sustainable society.

7.4.8 Legacy of Environmental Activism

Regardless of the outcome of his presidential campaign, Kennedy's legacy as an environmental activist and advocate for social justice will continue to shape the political landscape. His dedication to protecting the environment, promoting sustainable practices, and fighting for the rights of marginalized communities has left a lasting impact. Kennedy's work has inspired countless individuals to take action and has paved the way for future leaders to continue his environmental legacy.

In conclusion, Robert F. Kennedy Jr.'s presidential campaign in 2024 had a profound impact on the political landscape. His focus on environmental issues, social justice, and corporate accountability shifted the discourse, energized the environmental movement, and influenced the Democratic Party's agenda. Kennedy's campaign inspired future leaders and left a lasting legacy of environmental activism. Regardless of the outcome of his campaign, his contributions to the political landscape will continue to shape the future of environmental policy and advocacy.

8 Personal Life and Relationships

8.1 Marriage and Family

Robert F. Kennedy Jr. has had a rich and fulfilling personal life, marked by his marriage and the growth of his family. His commitment to his loved ones has been a source of strength and support throughout his environmental journey.

8.1.1 Marriage to Mary Richardson Kennedy

In 1994, Robert F. Kennedy Jr. married Mary Richardson, an accomplished architect and environmental activist. Their union was a testament to their shared values and commitment to making a positive impact on the world. Together, they had four children: Conor, Kyra, William, and Aiden.

8.1.2 Tragic Loss and Coping with Grief

Sadly, the Kennedy family faced a devastating loss when Mary Richardson Kennedy passed away in 2012. Her untimely death was a profound tragedy that deeply affected Robert and their children. Coping with grief and loss became an integral part of their journey, and Robert has spoken openly about the challenges and the importance of finding strength in difficult times.

8.1.3 Remarriage to Cheryl Hines

In 2014, Robert F. Kennedy Jr. remarried to Cheryl Hines, an accomplished actress and environmental advocate. Their marriage brought together two individuals who shared a passion for environmental causes and a desire to make a difference. Their union has been a source of happiness and stability for both Robert and Cheryl.

8.1.4 Parenting and Family Values

As a father, Robert F. Kennedy Jr. has instilled in his children a deep sense of responsibility towards the environment and the world around them. He has emphasized the importance of empathy, compassion, and taking action to protect the planet for future generations. Through his example, he has shown his children the power of using their voices and resources to effect positive change.

8.1.5 Balancing Personal and Professional Life

Like many individuals who are passionate about their work, Robert F. Kennedy Jr. has faced the challenge of balancing his personal and professional life. His dedication to environmental activism often requires him to travel extensively and engage in demanding advocacy work. However, he has made a conscious effort to prioritize his family and ensure that he is present for important milestones and moments in their lives.

8.1.6 Supportive Family Network

Robert F. Kennedy Jr. comes from a family with a long history of public service and activism. His family has been a constant source of support and inspiration throughout his environmental journey. The Kennedy family legacy, with its emphasis on social justice and making a difference, has undoubtedly influenced Robert's own values and commitment to creating a better world.

8.1.7 Philanthropic Endeavors

In addition to his environmental advocacy, Robert F. Kennedy Jr. has been involved in various philanthropic endeavors. He has used his resources and influence to support organizations and initiatives that align with his values and goals. Through his philanthropy, he has sought to address a wide range of social and environmental issues, furthering his commitment to creating a more just and sustainable world.

8.1.8 The Importance of Love and Support

Throughout his personal and professional journey, Robert F. Kennedy Jr. has emphasized the importance of love, support, and strong relationships. His marriage and family have provided him with a solid foundation from which to pursue his environmental activism. The love and support he receives from his family have undoubtedly played a significant role in his ability to navigate challenges, overcome obstacles, and continue his important work.

In the next section, we will explore Robert F. Kennedy Jr.'s personal interests and hobbies, shedding light on the diverse aspects of his life beyond his environmental activism.

[Continue to section 8.2: "Personal Interests and Hobbies"]

8.2 Personal Interests and Hobbies

Beyond his environmental activism and political endeavors, Robert F. Kennedy Jr. has a range of personal interests and hobbies that contribute to his well-rounded character. These pursuits provide him with a sense of balance and fulfillment outside of his professional life. They also offer insights into his personality and values.

8.2.1 Love for the Outdoors

One of Robert F. Kennedy Jr.'s greatest passions is spending time in nature. Growing up in a family that valued outdoor activities, he developed a deep appreciation for the environment and the beauty of the natural world. Kennedy often finds solace and inspiration in the great outdoors, whether it be hiking through forests, exploring national parks, or simply enjoying the tranquility of a peaceful beach.

8.2.2 Fly Fishing and Conservation

Fly fishing holds a special place in Kennedy's heart. He has been an avid angler for many years and sees it as a way to connect with nature on a deeper level. Through his love for fly fishing, Kennedy has also become a strong advocate for the conservation of rivers and waterways. He recognizes the importance of protecting these ecosystems and the delicate balance they maintain.

8.2.3 Photography and Visual Storytelling

Robert F. Kennedy Jr. has a keen eye for photography and uses this medium to capture the beauty of the natural world. His photographs often depict landscapes, wildlife, and environmental issues, serving as a powerful tool to raise awareness and inspire action. Through visual storytelling, Kennedy aims to convey the urgency of environmental conservation and the need for sustainable practices.

8.2.4 Writing and Journalism

As an accomplished author and journalist, Kennedy has a talent for writing and storytelling. He has written numerous articles and books on environmental issues, sharing his knowledge and experiences with a wide audience. Through his writing, Kennedy aims to educate and empower individuals to take action and make a positive impact on the environment.

8.2.5 Music and Songwriting

Music has always played a significant role in Kennedy's life. He is an accomplished guitar player and enjoys songwriting as a form of creative expression. Kennedy's love for music is deeply intertwined with his environmental activism, as he believes that music has the power to inspire change and unite people in the pursuit of a sustainable future.

8.2.6 Philanthropic Endeavors

In addition to his environmental work, Robert F. Kennedy Jr. is actively involved in various philanthropic endeavors. He supports organizations and initiatives that focus on social justice, human rights, and public health. Kennedy's philanthropic efforts reflect his commitment to creating a more equitable and sustainable world for all.

8.2.7 Family and Quality Time

Despite his busy schedule, Kennedy places great importance on spending quality time with his family. He cherishes moments with his children and values the opportunity to create lasting memories with them. Family gatherings and traditions hold a special place in his heart, as they provide a sense of connection and continuity in the midst of his demanding professional life.

8.2.8 Physical Fitness and Wellness

Maintaining physical fitness and overall wellness is essential to Kennedy's lifestyle. He recognizes the importance of taking care of his body and mind to sustain his energy and focus. Kennedy engages in regular exercise, such as running and yoga, to stay physically fit and maintain a healthy lifestyle. This commitment to wellness allows him to tackle the challenges of his environmental activism and political endeavors with vigor and resilience.

In conclusion, Robert F. Kennedy Jr. leads a multifaceted life beyond his environmental activism and political pursuits. His personal interests and hobbies reflect his deep connection to nature, his creative spirit, and his commitment to making a positive impact on the world. Through his love for the outdoors, fly fishing, photography, writing, music, philanthropy, and quality time with his family, Kennedy finds balance and fulfillment in his personal life, which in turn fuels his passion for environmental conservation and social justice.

8.3 Philanthropic Endeavors

Robert F. Kennedy Jr. has dedicated a significant portion of his life to philanthropic endeavors, using his resources and influence to make a positive impact on various social and environmental issues. His commitment to philanthropy stems from his deep-rooted belief in the importance of giving back to society and creating a better world for future generations.

8.3.1 Environmental Conservation

One of the primary areas of philanthropy for Robert F. Kennedy Jr. is environmental conservation. He has been actively involved in numerous organizations and initiatives aimed at protecting and preserving the natural world. Through his work with organizations like the Waterkeeper Alliance, Kennedy has been at the forefront of efforts to safeguard water bodies and promote clean water initiatives. His dedication to environmental conservation has led to the establishment of several successful programs and campaigns that have had a lasting impact on the protection of natural resources.

8.3.2 Public Health Advocacy

Recognizing the interconnectedness of the environment and public health, Robert F. Kennedy Jr. has also been involved in philanthropic endeavors related to public health advocacy. He has worked tirelessly to raise awareness about the adverse effects of environmental pollution on human health, particularly in marginalized communities. Kennedy has been a vocal advocate for environmental justice, fighting for equitable access to clean air, water, and a healthy environment for all individuals, regardless of their socioeconomic status.

8.3.3 Renewable Energy Initiatives

As a strong proponent of clean and sustainable energy sources, Robert F. Kennedy Jr. has actively supported and funded renewable energy initiatives. He believes that transitioning to renewable energy is not only crucial for mitigating climate change but also for creating a more sustainable and resilient future. Through his philanthropic efforts, Kennedy has contributed to the development and implementation of clean energy projects, such as solar and wind farms, that have helped reduce reliance on fossil fuels and promote a greener energy landscape.

8.3.4 Education and Youth Empowerment

Recognizing the importance of education in shaping the future, Robert F. Kennedy Jr. has also focused his philanthropic efforts on supporting educational initiatives and empowering youth. He believes that providing quality education and opportunities to young individuals is essential for creating a more just and sustainable society. Kennedy has been involved in various educational programs and initiatives that aim to bridge educational gaps, promote environmental literacy, and empower young people to become agents of change in their communities.

8.3.5 Social Justice and Human Rights

In addition to his environmental and educational philanthropy, Robert F. Kennedy Jr. has also been actively involved in supporting social justice and human rights causes. He has used his platform and resources to advocate for the rights of marginalized communities, fight against systemic injustices, and promote equality and inclusivity. Kennedy's philanthropic endeavors in this area have included supporting organizations that work towards ending racial discrimination, promoting gender equality, and advocating for the rights of indigenous peoples.

8.3.6 Collaborations and Partnerships

Robert F. Kennedy Jr. understands the power of collaboration and partnerships in achieving meaningful and lasting change. Throughout his philanthropic journey, he has actively sought out collaborations with like-minded individuals, organizations, and institutions to amplify the impact of his efforts. By joining forces with other philanthropists, activists, and experts, Kennedy has been able to leverage his resources and expertise to address complex social and environmental challenges more effectively.

8.3.7 Fundraising and Advocacy

In addition to his direct involvement in philanthropic initiatives, Robert F. Kennedy Jr. has also played a crucial role in fundraising and advocacy efforts. He has used his influence and public platform to raise awareness about various causes, mobilize support, and generate resources for organizations and projects aligned with his philanthropic goals. Kennedy's ability to effectively communicate and engage with diverse audiences has been instrumental in garnering support and driving positive change.

In conclusion, Robert F. Kennedy Jr.'s philanthropic endeavors have spanned a wide range of areas, including environmental conservation, public health advocacy, renewable energy initiatives, education, social justice, and human rights. Through his dedication and commitment to making a difference, he has left a lasting impact on numerous causes and has inspired others to join the fight for a more sustainable and just world. Kennedy's philanthropy serves as a testament to his belief in the power of collective action and his unwavering commitment to creating a better future for all.

8.4 Balancing Personal and Professional Life

Balancing personal and professional life is a challenge that many individuals face, and Robert F. Kennedy Jr. is no exception. As a prominent environmental activist, lawyer, and author, Kennedy has dedicated a significant portion of his life to advocating for environmental causes and fighting for justice. However, he also recognizes the importance of maintaining a fulfilling personal life and nurturing relationships with his loved ones.

8.4.1 Prioritizing Family and Relationships

Despite his demanding schedule and numerous commitments, Kennedy places a high value on his family and relationships. He understands that maintaining strong connections with his loved ones is essential for his overall well-being and happiness. Kennedy has been married twice and has six children, whom he cherishes dearly. He strives to spend quality time with his family, creating lasting memories and fostering a sense of togetherness.

Kennedy's commitment to his family is evident in his efforts to be present for important milestones and events in their lives. He actively participates in his children's activities and supports their endeavors. By prioritizing his family, Kennedy demonstrates that personal relationships are a vital aspect of his life that he refuses to neglect.

8.4.2 Carving Out Personal Time

In addition to his family, Kennedy recognizes the importance of personal time and self-care. He understands that taking care of his physical and mental well-being is crucial for maintaining the energy and focus required for his professional endeavors. Kennedy engages in various activities that bring him joy and help him recharge.

One of Kennedy's passions is spending time in nature. He finds solace in outdoor activities such as hiking, fishing, and sailing. These activities not only allow him to connect with the environment he fights to protect but also provide him with a sense of peace and rejuvenation.

Furthermore, Kennedy is an avid reader and writer. He values the power of literature and often immerses himself in books that expand his knowledge and understanding of the world. Writing is also a form of personal expression for Kennedy, allowing him to reflect on his experiences and share his insights with others.

8.4.3 Seeking Support and Delegation

Recognizing the limitations of his time and energy, Kennedy understands the importance of seeking support and delegating tasks. He surrounds himself with a team of dedicated individuals who share his passion for environmental activism and assist him in various aspects of his work. By delegating responsibilities, Kennedy can focus on the areas where his expertise and influence are most needed.

Moreover, Kennedy actively seeks support from his loved ones and professional network. He understands that he cannot accomplish everything alone and relies on the collective efforts of like-minded individuals to make a significant impact. By building a strong support system, Kennedy ensures that he has the necessary resources and assistance to navigate the challenges of balancing personal and professional life.

8.4.4 Maintaining Boundaries and Priorities

Balancing personal and professional life requires setting boundaries and establishing priorities. Kennedy understands that he cannot be everywhere at once and must make choices that align with his values and goals. He carefully selects the causes and projects he commits to, ensuring that they align with his mission and have the potential for meaningful impact.

Kennedy also recognizes the importance of setting boundaries to protect his personal time and well-being. He understands that saying no to certain commitments is necessary to maintain a healthy work-life balance. By setting clear boundaries, Kennedy ensures that he can dedicate time and energy to both his personal life and his professional endeavors without compromising either.

In conclusion, Robert F. Kennedy Jr. understands the significance of balancing personal and professional life. Despite his demanding schedule and numerous commitments, he prioritizes his family and relationships, carves out personal time for self-care, seeks support and delegation, and maintains boundaries and priorities. By striking a balance between his personal and professional life, Kennedy is able to lead a fulfilling and purposeful existence while making a significant impact in the field of environmental activism.

9 Legacy and Influence

9.1 Impact on Environmental Movement

Robert F. Kennedy Jr. has had a profound impact on the environmental movement, leaving a lasting legacy that continues to inspire and drive change. Through his tireless advocacy, he has brought attention to critical environmental issues, championed the protection of natural resources, and fought for environmental justice and equity. Kennedy's contributions have not only shaped policy and legislation but have also inspired individuals and organizations to take action and make a difference.

9.1.1 Environmental Advocacy and Awareness

One of the most significant impacts of Robert F. Kennedy Jr.'s environmental journey has been his ability to raise awareness about pressing environmental issues. Through his speeches, writings, and public appearances, he has effectively communicated the urgency of addressing climate change, protecting biodiversity, and preserving our natural resources. Kennedy's ability to articulate complex environmental problems in a relatable manner has helped engage a broader audience and mobilize support for environmental causes.

Kennedy's work with the Waterkeeper Alliance, an organization he co-founded, has been instrumental in protecting waterways and promoting clean water initiatives. By advocating for the enforcement of environmental laws and regulations, he has held polluters accountable and ensured the preservation of vital ecosystems. His efforts have not only improved water quality but have also inspired similar initiatives around the world.

9.1.2 Policy and Legislative Impact

Robert F. Kennedy Jr.'s influence on environmental policy and legislation cannot be overstated. Through his extensive knowledge and expertise, he has played a crucial role in shaping environmental laws and regulations. Kennedy has worked tirelessly to promote clean energy initiatives, advocating for the transition to renewable sources and the reduction of greenhouse gas emissions.

His involvement in landmark environmental lawsuits, such as the case against General Electric for the contamination of the Hudson River, has set important legal precedents and established the responsibility of corporations to protect the environment. Kennedy's legal expertise and commitment to justice have been instrumental in holding polluters accountable and ensuring the enforcement of environmental regulations.

9.1.3 Environmental Justice and Equity

Robert F. Kennedy Jr. has been a vocal advocate for environmental justice and equity, recognizing that marginalized communities often bear the brunt of environmental degradation. He has fought against environmental racism, highlighting the disproportionate impact of pollution and environmental hazards on low-income communities and communities of color.

Kennedy's work has shed light on the intersectionality of environmental issues with social and economic disparities. By amplifying the voices of those affected by environmental injustices, he has brought attention to the need for inclusive and equitable environmental policies. His advocacy has helped bridge the gap between environmentalism and social justice, inspiring a more holistic approach to addressing environmental challenges.

9.1.4 Inspiring Action and Mobilizing Change

One of the most significant contributions of Robert F. Kennedy Jr. to the environmental movement has been his ability to inspire individuals and organizations to take action. Through his passion, knowledge, and unwavering commitment, he has motivated countless people to become environmental stewards and advocates for change.

Kennedy's ability to connect with diverse audiences, from policymakers to grassroots activists, has been instrumental in mobilizing support for environmental causes. His speeches and writings have provided a roadmap for individuals and communities to engage in sustainable practices, promote renewable energy, and protect the environment. By leading by example, Kennedy has shown that everyone has a role to play in creating a more sustainable future.

9.1.5 Collaboration and Partnerships

Robert F. Kennedy Jr.'s impact on the environmental movement extends beyond his individual efforts. He has been instrumental in fostering collaboration and partnerships among various stakeholders, including government agencies, non-profit organizations, and grassroots movements.

Kennedy's ability to bridge divides and find common ground has facilitated the development of innovative solutions to environmental challenges. By bringing together experts from different fields and sectors, he has encouraged interdisciplinary approaches to environmental problem-solving. His collaborative approach has not only strengthened the environmental movement but has also fostered a sense of collective responsibility and shared purpose.

In conclusion, Robert F. Kennedy Jr.'s impact on the environmental movement has been profound and far-reaching. Through his advocacy, policy work, and ability to inspire action, he has shaped the discourse around environmental issues and mobilized individuals and organizations to work towards a more sustainable future. Kennedy's legacy will continue to influence and inspire future generations of environmental activists, ensuring that his green legacy lives on.

9.2 Inspiring Future Generations

Robert F. Kennedy Jr.'s environmental journey has not only left a lasting impact on the world but has also inspired future generations to take action and make a difference. Through his tireless advocacy, unwavering commitment, and groundbreaking achievements, Kennedy has become a beacon of hope for those who believe in the power of individuals to effect change. His passion for the environment and his dedication to protecting it have resonated with people from all walks of life, inspiring them to follow in his footsteps and become environmental stewards themselves.

9.2.1 A Role Model for Environmental Activism

Kennedy's unwavering dedication to environmental activism has made him a role model for aspiring environmentalists. His ability to combine his legal expertise with his passion for the environment has set him apart as a leader in the field. By using the law as a tool for change, Kennedy has shown future generations that they too can make a difference by leveraging their skills and knowledge to protect the planet.

9.2.2 Educating and Empowering Youth

One of Kennedy's most significant contributions to inspiring future generations is his focus on educating and empowering youth. He understands that young people are the key to a sustainable future and has made it his mission to engage and educate them about environmental issues. Through his speeches, interviews, and outreach programs, Kennedy has encouraged young people to become active participants in the fight against climate change and environmental degradation.

Kennedy has also been instrumental in establishing educational initiatives that aim to inspire and empower young environmentalists. For example, he has been involved in the creation of environmental education programs in schools and universities, providing students with the knowledge and tools they need to become effective advocates for the environment. By investing in the education of future generations, Kennedy has ensured that his legacy will continue long after he is gone.

9.2.3 Encouraging Civic Engagement

Kennedy's advocacy work has not only inspired individuals to take action but has also encouraged civic engagement on a larger scale. Through his campaigns and initiatives, he has shown people that their voices matter and that they have the power to influence policy and effect change. By engaging with communities, organizing grassroots movements, and mobilizing support, Kennedy has demonstrated the importance of active citizenship in shaping a sustainable future.

9.2.4 Bridging Divides and Building Coalitions

Kennedy's ability to bridge divides and build coalitions has been instrumental in inspiring future generations to work together for a common cause. He has shown that environmental issues transcend political affiliations and that collaboration is essential in finding solutions. By reaching across party lines and working with individuals and organizations from diverse backgrounds, Kennedy has demonstrated the power of unity in achieving environmental goals.

9.2.5 Leading by Example

Perhaps one of the most inspiring aspects of Kennedy's environmental journey is his ability to lead by example. He has consistently demonstrated his commitment to sustainable practices in his personal life, from driving electric vehicles to installing solar panels on his properties. By living in alignment with his values, Kennedy has shown others that it is possible to make a difference through individual actions.

9.2.6 Inspiring Hope and Resilience

Kennedy's unwavering optimism and resilience in the face of environmental challenges have inspired hope in countless individuals. Despite the daunting nature of the issues at hand, Kennedy has consistently emphasized the importance of hope and the belief that change is possible. His ability to inspire others to stay committed and continue fighting for a better future has been a driving force behind the growth of the environmental movement.

9.2.7 Mentoring the Next Generation

Kennedy has taken an active role in mentoring and supporting the next generation of environmental leaders. Through mentorship programs, internships, and speaking engagements, he has provided guidance and support to young activists, helping them navigate the complexities of environmental advocacy. By sharing his experiences and knowledge, Kennedy has empowered young leaders to carry on his legacy and continue the fight for a sustainable future.

9.2.8 Embracing Innovation and Technology

Kennedy's embrace of innovation and technology has also inspired future generations to explore new solutions to environmental challenges. He has been a vocal advocate for clean energy and has championed the use of renewable resources as a means of combating climate change. By highlighting the potential of technology in creating a sustainable future, Kennedy has encouraged young innovators to develop and implement groundbreaking solutions.

9.2.9 Promoting Diversity and Inclusion

Kennedy has been a strong advocate for diversity and inclusion within the environmental movement. He recognizes that environmental issues disproportionately affect marginalized communities and has worked to amplify their voices and ensure their inclusion in decision-making processes. By promoting diversity and inclusion, Kennedy has inspired future generations to approach environmental activism with an intersectional lens, recognizing the interconnectedness of social and environmental justice.

9.2.10 Fostering a Sense of Urgency

Above all, Kennedy's work has instilled a sense of urgency in future generations. He has consistently emphasized the need for immediate action to address pressing environmental issues, such as climate change and pollution. By highlighting the consequences of inaction and the potential for a sustainable future, Kennedy has motivated individuals to take action now, rather than waiting for others to solve the problems at hand.

In conclusion, Robert F. Kennedy Jr.'s environmental journey has inspired future generations to become active participants in the fight for a sustainable future. Through his leadership, advocacy, and commitment to education, Kennedy has empowered individuals to make a difference and has shown them that their actions can have a lasting impact. His legacy will continue to inspire and guide environmental activists for years to come, ensuring that his green legacy lives on.

9.3 Continuing the Kennedy Legacy

The Kennedy family has a long-standing legacy of public service and activism, and Robert F. Kennedy Jr. has continued this tradition by dedicating his life to environmental advocacy. As the son of Robert F. Kennedy, a prominent political figure who was tragically assassinated in 1968, Robert F. Kennedy Jr. has not only carried on his father's name but also his commitment to making a positive impact on the world.

9.3.1 Upholding the Values of Public Service

Robert F. Kennedy Jr. has been deeply influenced by his family's commitment to public service. Growing up in a household that valued social justice and equality, he witnessed firsthand the power of using one's platform to advocate for positive change. This upbringing instilled in him a strong sense of duty and a desire to make a difference in the world.

Continuing the Kennedy legacy means upholding the values of public service, which Robert F. Kennedy Jr. has done through his environmental activism. By dedicating his career to protecting the environment and advocating for sustainable practices, he has demonstrated a commitment to the greater good and the well-being of future generations.

9.3.2 Environmental Advocacy as a Family Tradition

The Kennedy family has a history of environmental activism, and Robert F. Kennedy Jr. has carried this torch forward. His father, Robert F. Kennedy, was a strong advocate for environmental conservation and played a key role in the creation of national parks and the protection of natural resources. This familial influence has undoubtedly shaped Robert F. Kennedy Jr.'s own passion for environmental issues.

By continuing the Kennedy legacy, Robert F. Kennedy Jr. has not only honored his family's commitment to public service but also expanded upon it. Through his work with organizations like the Waterkeeper Alliance, he has actively fought for clean water and the preservation of ecosystems. His dedication to environmental causes has not only raised awareness but has also inspired others to take action.

9.3.3 Inspiring Future Generations

One of the most significant aspects of continuing the Kennedy legacy is inspiring future generations to get involved in public service and environmental activism. Robert F. Kennedy Jr.'s work has served as a source of inspiration for many young individuals who are passionate about making a difference in the world.

Through his speeches, interviews, and public appearances, Robert F. Kennedy Jr. has shared his knowledge and experiences, encouraging others to take up the cause of environmental conservation. By highlighting the urgency of the issues at hand and providing tangible solutions, he has motivated countless individuals to become active participants in the fight against climate change and environmental degradation.

9.3.4 Education and Awareness

Continuing the Kennedy legacy also involves educating and raising awareness about environmental issues. Robert F. Kennedy Jr. has been instrumental in this regard, using his platform to inform the public about the consequences of environmental degradation and the importance of sustainable practices.

Through his books, articles, and public engagements, Robert F. Kennedy Jr. has provided valuable insights into the complex relationship between human activities and the environment. By presenting scientific evidence and real-life examples, he has helped people understand the urgency of the environmental crisis and the need for immediate action.

9.3.5 Collaboration and Partnerships

Continuing the Kennedy legacy requires collaboration and partnerships with like-minded individuals and organizations. Robert F. Kennedy Jr. has actively sought out alliances with environmental activists, scientists, policymakers, and community leaders to amplify his impact and effect meaningful change.

By working together with diverse stakeholders, Robert F. Kennedy Jr. has been able to advocate for stronger environmental policies, promote sustainable practices, and protect natural resources. His ability to build bridges and foster cooperation has been instrumental in advancing the environmental movement and ensuring a sustainable future for all.

9.3.6 Empowering the Next Generation of Leaders

As part of continuing the Kennedy legacy, Robert F. Kennedy Jr. has focused on empowering the next generation of leaders. He has mentored and supported young activists, providing them with the tools and resources they need to make a difference in their communities.

Through initiatives such as the Waterkeeper Alliance's Youth Programs, Robert F. Kennedy Jr. has encouraged young people to become environmental stewards and take an active role in shaping the future. By nurturing their passion and providing them with opportunities for growth, he has ensured that the Kennedy legacy will live on through the actions of future leaders.

9.3.7 The Enduring Impact of Robert F. Kennedy Jr.

Robert F. Kennedy Jr.'s contributions to the environmental movement have had a lasting impact. His advocacy for clean energy, protection of natural resources, and promotion of sustainable practices has influenced policy decisions, shaped public opinion, and inspired countless individuals to take action.

By continuing the Kennedy legacy, Robert F. Kennedy Jr. has left a profound imprint on the environmental movement. His dedication to the cause, his ability to mobilize support, and his unwavering commitment to justice and truth have made him a respected figure in the fight against climate change and environmental injustice.

As we look to the future, it is clear that Robert F. Kennedy Jr.'s legacy will continue to inspire and guide generations to come. His work serves as a reminder that each individual has the power to make a difference and that the fight for a sustainable and just world is a collective responsibility.

9.4 Long-Term Influence and Recognition

Throughout his life and career, Robert F. Kennedy Jr. has made a significant impact on the environmental movement and has been recognized for his contributions and achievements. His tireless advocacy for environmental justice, clean energy, and the protection of natural resources has earned him both admiration and respect from individuals and organizations around the world. Kennedy's long-term influence and recognition can be seen in various aspects of his work and the lasting impact he has had on the environmental movement.

9.4.1 Environmental Movement and Policy

One of the most significant ways in which Robert F. Kennedy Jr. has left a lasting influence is through his contributions to the environmental movement. As the founder of the Waterkeeper Alliance, Kennedy has played a crucial role in the protection and preservation of water bodies worldwide. His efforts have led to the establishment of numerous Waterkeeper organizations, which work tirelessly to monitor and safeguard rivers, lakes, and coastlines.

Kennedy's work has also had a profound impact on environmental policy and legislation. Through his advocacy and expertise, he has influenced the development and implementation of various environmental laws and regulations. His involvement in landmark cases, such as the Hudson Riverkeeper lawsuit, has set important legal precedents and helped shape environmental policy in the United States.

9.4.2 Public Awareness and Education

Another aspect of Kennedy's long-term influence is his ability to raise public awareness about environmental issues. Through his speeches, interviews, and public appearances, he has effectively communicated the urgency of addressing environmental challenges and the need for sustainable practices.

Kennedy's ability to articulate complex environmental concepts in a relatable manner has helped educate and inspire individuals from all walks of life.

Kennedy's efforts to promote environmental education have also had a lasting impact. He has been actively involved in educational initiatives, including the development of environmental curricula for schools and universities. By emphasizing the importance of environmental stewardship and providing resources for educators, Kennedy has helped shape the minds of future generations and instilled a sense of responsibility towards the environment.

9.4.3 Global Recognition and Awards

Robert F. Kennedy Jr.'s contributions to the environmental movement have not gone unnoticed. He has received numerous awards and accolades for his work, further solidifying his long-term influence and recognition. Kennedy has been honored with prestigious awards such as the United Nations Champions of the Earth Award and the Goldman Environmental Prize. These accolades highlight his significant contributions to environmental conservation and his dedication to creating a sustainable future.

Additionally, Kennedy's work has been recognized by various organizations and institutions. He has been invited to speak at international conferences and events, where his expertise and insights have been sought after by policymakers, scientists, and environmentalists. Kennedy's influence extends beyond national borders, as he has collaborated with global organizations to address environmental challenges on a global scale.

9.4.4 Inspiring Future Generations

One of the most profound aspects of Robert F. Kennedy Jr.'s long-term influence is his ability to inspire and motivate future generations. Through his passion, dedication, and unwavering commitment to environmental causes, he has become a role model for aspiring environmentalists and activists. Kennedy's ability to connect with people from diverse backgrounds and engage them in environmental issues has sparked a renewed interest in environmental activism.

Kennedy's influence can be seen in the emergence of a new generation of environmental leaders who have been inspired by his work. Many individuals have been motivated to pursue careers in environmental science, policy, and advocacy due to Kennedy's impact. His ability to mobilize and empower young people has created a ripple effect, leading to a broader and more diverse environmental movement.

9.4.5 Legacy and Enduring Impact

Robert F. Kennedy Jr.'s long-term influence and recognition can be seen in the enduring impact of his work. His contributions to the environmental movement have laid the foundation for continued progress and change. The organizations he has founded, such as the Waterkeeper Alliance, will continue to protect and preserve water bodies for generations to come.

Kennedy's advocacy for clean energy and sustainable practices has also had a lasting impact on the transition towards a greener future. His efforts to promote renewable energy sources and reduce reliance on fossil fuels have influenced policy decisions and shaped public opinion. The shift towards clean energy and sustainable practices is a testament to Kennedy's enduring legacy.

Furthermore, Kennedy's outspoken views on the murder of his father, Senator Robert F. Kennedy, have shed light on the importance of seeking justice and truth. His advocacy for a thorough investigation and his commitment to uncovering the truth have resonated with many individuals who share his desire for transparency and accountability.

In conclusion, Robert F. Kennedy Jr.'s long-term influence and recognition can be seen in his contributions to the environmental movement, his ability to raise public awareness, the global recognition and awards he has received, his inspiration of future generations, and the enduring impact of his work.

Kennedy's legacy will continue to shape the environmental movement and inspire individuals to take action for a more sustainable and just world.

10 Lessons and Reflections

10.1 Lessons Learned from Robert F. Kennedy Jr.

Throughout his life and career, Robert F. Kennedy Jr. has imparted valuable lessons that have resonated with individuals from all walks of life. His unwavering commitment to environmental activism and his dedication to fighting for justice and truth have left a lasting impact on those who have followed his journey. Here are some of the key lessons we can learn from Robert F. Kennedy Jr.:

10.1.1 The Power of Family and Legacy

One of the most significant lessons we can learn from Robert F. Kennedy Jr. is the power of family and the impact of a strong legacy. Growing up as part of the Kennedy family, he was surrounded by a tradition of public service and a commitment to making a difference in the world. The influence of his family played a crucial role in shaping his values and instilling in him a sense of responsibility to protect the environment and fight for justice.

10.1.2 The Importance of Environmental Stewardship

Robert F. Kennedy Jr.'s environmental activism has taught us the importance of being good stewards of the environment. He has consistently emphasized the need to protect our natural resources, promote sustainable practices, and combat climate change. His work has highlighted the interconnectedness of environmental issues and the urgent need for collective action to preserve the planet for future generations.

10.1.3 Courage to Speak Truth to Power

One of the most admirable qualities of Robert F. Kennedy Jr. is his courage to speak truth to power. He has fearlessly challenged corporate interests and government policies that harm the environment and endanger public health. His willingness to confront powerful entities and hold them accountable has inspired others to stand up for what they believe in and fight for justice, even in the face of opposition.

10.1.4 The Pursuit of Environmental Justice

Robert F. Kennedy Jr.'s advocacy for environmental justice has taught us the importance of addressing the disproportionate impact of environmental issues on marginalized communities. He has consistently fought for equal access to clean air, water, and a healthy environment for all. His work has shed light on the intersectionality of environmental issues with social and economic inequalities, inspiring a broader movement for environmental justice.

10.1.5 The Power of Collaboration and Grassroots Activism

Another valuable lesson we can learn from Robert F. Kennedy Jr. is the power of collaboration and grassroots activism. He has been instrumental in founding organizations like the Waterkeeper Alliance, which brings together local communities, activists, and legal experts to protect waterways. His work has shown that collective action and community engagement are essential for creating meaningful change and holding polluters accountable.

10.1.6 The Importance of Science and Evidence-Based Decision Making

Robert F. Kennedy Jr.'s advocacy has underscored the importance of relying on science and evidence-based decision making when addressing environmental issues. He has consistently emphasized the need to base policies and regulations on sound scientific research and data. His commitment to truth and accuracy has been instrumental in debunking misinformation and ensuring that environmental decisions are grounded in facts.

10.1.7 Resilience in the Face of Opposition

Robert F. Kennedy Jr.'s journey has taught us the importance of resilience in the face of opposition. Throughout his career, he has faced criticism, attacks, and attempts to discredit his work. However, he has remained steadfast in his commitment to his principles and has continued to advocate for environmental causes despite the challenges. His resilience serves as an inspiration to persevere in the face of adversity and to never give up on fighting for what is right.

10.1.8 The Power of Education and Awareness

Robert F. Kennedy Jr.'s work has highlighted the power of education and awareness in driving change. He has consistently emphasized the need to educate ourselves and others about environmental issues, their impact, and potential solutions. By raising awareness and empowering individuals with knowledge, he has inspired countless people to take action and make a positive difference in their communities.

10.1.9 The Importance of Balancing Personal and Professional Life

Robert F. Kennedy Jr.'s life serves as a reminder of the importance of balancing personal and professional life. Despite his demanding career and advocacy work, he has prioritized his family, personal interests, and philanthropic endeavors. His ability to find harmony between his personal and professional life serves as a valuable lesson for individuals striving to make a difference while maintaining a fulfilling personal life.

10.1.10 The Need for Long-Term Vision and Persistence

Finally, Robert F. Kennedy Jr.'s journey has taught us the need for a long-term vision and persistence in achieving meaningful change. He has consistently emphasized that environmental issues require sustained effort and a commitment to long-term solutions. His work serves as a reminder that progress may take time, but with persistence and dedication, we can create a better and more sustainable future.

In conclusion, Robert F. Kennedy Jr.'s life and accomplishments have provided valuable lessons for individuals passionate about environmental activism, justice, and truth. From the power of family and legacy to the importance of collaboration, resilience, and evidence-based decision making, his journey serves as an inspiration for future generations to continue the fight for a greener and more just world.

10.2 Reflections on Environmental Activism

Throughout his environmental journey, Robert F. Kennedy Jr. has dedicated his life to advocating for the protection of the environment and the promotion of sustainable practices. His work has been driven by a deep passion for the natural world and a belief in the importance of preserving it for future generations. As he reflects on his environmental activism, Kennedy Jr. recognizes both the progress that has been made and the challenges that lie ahead.

10.2.1 Progress and Achievements

Kennedy Jr. acknowledges the significant progress that has been made in the field of environmental activism. He has witnessed the passing of important environmental policies and legislation that have helped to protect natural resources, promote clean energy initiatives, and address the impacts of climate change. He takes pride in the accomplishments of organizations like the Waterkeeper Alliance, which he co-founded, and the positive impact they have had on water quality and environmental conservation.

Kennedy Jr. also recognizes the power of grassroots movements and the role they have played in raising awareness and driving change. He has witnessed communities coming together to fight against environmental injustices and corporate influence on the environment. These collective efforts have led to victories in the form of legal victories, improved regulations, and increased public awareness.

10.2.2 Challenges and Obstacles

Despite the progress that has been made, Kennedy Jr. acknowledges that there are still significant challenges and obstacles to overcome in the realm of environmental activism. He recognizes the need for continued advocacy and the importance of holding corporations and governments accountable for their actions. He understands that the fight for environmental justice and sustainability is an ongoing battle that requires constant vigilance.

One of the major challenges Kennedy Jr. faces is the opposition and criticism he receives from those who disagree with his views and his environmental activism. He has been the target of misinformation campaigns and personal attacks, which he believes are attempts to discredit his work and undermine the environmental movement as a whole. However, he remains steadfast in his commitment to the cause and continues to advocate for change.

10.2.3 The Importance of Education and Awareness

Kennedy Jr. emphasizes the importance of education and awareness in driving environmental change. He believes that by educating individuals about the impact of their actions on the environment, they can make informed choices and take steps to reduce their ecological footprint. He advocates for environmental education to be integrated into school curricula and for individuals to be empowered with the knowledge and tools to make sustainable choices.

Kennedy Jr. also recognizes the power of storytelling and communication in raising awareness about environmental issues. He believes that by sharing stories of environmental successes and challenges, individuals can be inspired to take action and make a difference. He has used his platform as an author and public speaker to share his own experiences and to amplify the voices of those fighting for environmental justice.

10.2.4 Collaboration and Collective Action

Kennedy Jr. emphasizes the importance of collaboration and collective action in addressing environmental challenges. He believes that by working together, individuals, communities, and organizations can have a greater impact than they would on their own. He encourages partnerships between environmental organizations, businesses, and governments to find innovative solutions to environmental problems.

Kennedy Jr. also recognizes the need for diverse perspectives and voices in the environmental movement. He believes that by including a wide range of stakeholders, including marginalized communities, in decision-making processes, more equitable and effective solutions can be found. He advocates for the inclusion of indigenous knowledge and practices in environmental conservation efforts, recognizing the wisdom and sustainability of traditional ecological knowledge.

10.2.5 The Importance of Hope and Resilience

In the face of the immense challenges posed by climate change and environmental degradation, Kennedy Jr. emphasizes the importance of maintaining hope and resilience. He believes that despite the dire state of the planet, there is still time to make a difference and create a more sustainable future. He encourages individuals to take action, no matter how small, and to believe in the power of collective efforts to effect change.

Kennedy Jr. also recognizes the need for self-care and personal well-being in the pursuit of environmental activism. He acknowledges the emotional toll that fighting for the environment can take and encourages individuals to find balance in their lives. He believes that by taking care of oneself, individuals can sustain their passion and commitment to the cause in the long term.

In conclusion, Robert F. Kennedy Jr. reflects on his environmental activism with a sense of pride for the progress that has been made, but also with a recognition of the challenges that lie ahead. He emphasizes the importance of education, collaboration, and hope in driving environmental change. Despite the opposition he faces and the obstacles that exist, Kennedy Jr. remains committed to his mission of protecting the environment and inspiring future generations to do the same.

10.3 Personal Growth and Evolution

Throughout his life and career, Robert F. Kennedy Jr. has undergone significant personal growth and evolution. His journey as an environmental activist and advocate has shaped his beliefs, values, and perspectives, leading to a deeper understanding of the interconnectedness between environmental issues, social justice, and public health. Kennedy's personal growth can be seen in his evolving approach to environmental activism, his commitment to justice and truth, and his ability to navigate controversies and opposition.

10.3.1 Evolving Approach to Environmental Activism

Robert F. Kennedy Jr.'s early experiences and exposure to environmental issues laid the foundation for his lifelong commitment to environmental activism. However, his approach to advocacy has evolved over time. Initially, Kennedy focused on legal battles and environmental lawsuits, using the power of the law to hold polluters accountable. As he delved deeper into the complexities of environmental issues, he recognized the need for a more holistic approach.

Kennedy's evolution as an environmental activist led him to found the Waterkeeper Alliance, a global movement dedicated to protecting waterways and ensuring clean water for all. Through this organization, he emphasized the importance of community engagement, grassroots activism, and collaboration with local communities. Kennedy's shift towards a more community-centered approach reflects his understanding that environmental issues cannot be solved in isolation but require the active participation of individuals and communities.

10.3.2 Commitment to Justice and Truth

The murder of his father, Senator Robert F. Kennedy, had a profound impact on Robert F. Kennedy Jr.'s life and career. It fueled his commitment to seeking justice and truth, not only for his father but also for the marginalized and oppressed. Kennedy has been a vocal advocate for justice, tirelessly working to uncover the truth behind his father's assassination and challenging the official narrative.

Kennedy's pursuit of justice extends beyond his personal experiences. He has been a staunch advocate for environmental justice, highlighting the disproportionate impact of pollution and environmental degradation on marginalized communities. His belief in the inherent right of every individual to a clean and healthy environment has driven his efforts to address environmental inequalities and fight for the rights of those most affected by environmental harm.

10.3.3 Navigating Controversies and Opposition

As a prominent environmental activist, Robert F. Kennedy Jr. has faced his fair share of controversies and opposition. His outspoken views and advocacy have made him a target for critics who question his motives and challenge his credibility. However, Kennedy has demonstrated resilience and an ability to navigate these challenges with grace and determination.

In the face of opposition, Kennedy has consistently relied on facts, scientific evidence, and rigorous research to support his arguments. He has been proactive in debunking misinformation and addressing misconceptions about his work. Kennedy's commitment to transparency and accountability has helped him maintain credibility and effectively counter the attacks and criticisms directed towards him.

10.3.4 Growth and Adaptation in the Political Landscape

Robert F. Kennedy Jr.'s decision to run for President in 2024 reflects his growth and adaptation to the political landscape. While he has been primarily known for his environmental activism, Kennedy recognizes the need for systemic change and believes that political leadership is crucial in addressing the pressing challenges of our time.

His presidential campaign is a testament to his evolution as a leader and his desire to effect change on a broader scale. Kennedy's campaign platform and policy proposals reflect his comprehensive understanding of the interconnectedness between environmental issues, social justice, and public health. He aims to address climate change, promote clean energy initiatives, and advocate for environmental justice, among other key priorities.

Kennedy's run for President in 2024 also signifies his willingness to engage in the political arena and work within the existing system to drive meaningful change. It demonstrates his growth as a leader and his recognition of the importance of political power in shaping policies and influencing decision-making processes.

In conclusion, Robert F. Kennedy Jr.'s personal growth and evolution have been instrumental in shaping his environmental activism, his commitment to justice and truth, and his ability to navigate controversies and opposition. His evolving approach to environmental advocacy, his unwavering pursuit of justice, and his adaptability in the political landscape demonstrate his growth as a leader and his dedication to creating a more sustainable and just world. Kennedy's personal journey serves as an inspiration for individuals and future generations, highlighting the importance of continuous growth, learning, and adaptation in the pursuit of positive change.

10.4 Future Challenges and Opportunities

As Robert F. Kennedy Jr. continues his environmental journey, he faces both challenges and opportunities in his pursuit of a sustainable and just world. The future holds a range of complex issues that require innovative solutions and collective action. In this section, we will explore some of the key challenges and opportunities that lie ahead for Kennedy and the broader environmental movement.

10.4.1 Climate Change and Global Crisis

One of the most pressing challenges facing humanity is the escalating threat of climate change. Rising global temperatures, extreme weather events, and the loss of biodiversity pose significant risks to ecosystems, communities, and economies worldwide. Kennedy recognizes the urgency of addressing this crisis and has been a vocal advocate for climate action.

In the coming years, Kennedy will continue to push for ambitious policies and initiatives to mitigate greenhouse gas emissions, transition to clean energy sources, and promote sustainable practices. He will work towards building a global consensus on climate change and fostering international cooperation to tackle this existential threat.

10.4.2 Environmental Justice and Equity

Environmental justice remains a critical issue that demands attention and action. Low-income communities and marginalized groups often bear the brunt of environmental degradation and pollution. Kennedy has been a staunch advocate for environmental justice, fighting for equitable access to clean air, water, and a healthy environment for all.

In the future, Kennedy will strive to address the disproportionate impacts of environmental harm on vulnerable communities. He will work towards dismantling systemic inequalities and ensuring that environmental policies and initiatives prioritize the needs and rights of marginalized populations.

10.4.3 Corporate Influence and Accountability

The influence of corporations on environmental policy and regulation is a significant challenge that Kennedy will continue to confront. Powerful industries often prioritize profit over environmental sustainability, leading to the exploitation of natural resources and the degradation of ecosystems. Kennedy has been a vocal critic of corporate influence on the environment and has fought against the undue influence of polluting industries.

Moving forward, Kennedy will advocate for greater corporate accountability and transparency. He will work towards strengthening regulations, reducing corporate lobbying, and promoting sustainable business practices. By holding corporations accountable for their environmental impact, Kennedy aims to create a more sustainable and responsible business landscape.

10.4.4 Technological Innovation and Solutions

The advancement of technology presents both challenges and opportunities in the environmental realm. While technological innovations have the potential to drive sustainable development and conservation efforts, they also come with risks and uncertainties. Kennedy recognizes the need to harness the power of technology for positive environmental change while ensuring that it is used responsibly and ethically.

In the future, Kennedy will continue to explore and promote innovative solutions to environmental challenges. He will support research and development in clean energy technologies, sustainable agriculture, and conservation practices. By embracing technological advancements, Kennedy aims to accelerate the transition to a more sustainable and resilient future.

10.4.5 Collaboration and Grassroots Movements

Addressing complex environmental issues requires collaboration and collective action. Kennedy understands the importance of grassroots movements and community engagement in driving meaningful change. He has been a strong proponent of citizen activism and has worked closely with environmental organizations and communities to advocate for environmental protection.

In the years to come, Kennedy will continue to foster collaboration and empower grassroots movements. He will support community-led initiatives, encourage citizen participation, and amplify the voices of those affected by environmental injustices. By building strong alliances and mobilizing collective action, Kennedy aims to create a powerful force for environmental change.

10.4.6 Education and Awareness

Education and awareness play a crucial role in shaping public opinion and driving environmental action. Kennedy recognizes the need to educate and inspire individuals to become environmental stewards. He has been actively involved in raising awareness about environmental issues through public speaking engagements, interviews, and writing.

In the future, Kennedy will continue to prioritize education and awareness as key tools for environmental advocacy. He will work towards expanding environmental education programs, promoting scientific literacy, and fostering a deeper understanding of the interconnectedness between human well-being and the environment. By empowering individuals with knowledge, Kennedy aims to create a more informed and engaged society.

In conclusion, the future holds both challenges and opportunities for Robert F. Kennedy Jr. and his environmental journey. Climate change, environmental justice, corporate influence, technological innovation, collaboration, and education will be key areas of focus. By addressing these challenges and seizing opportunities, Kennedy aims to leave a lasting legacy of environmental stewardship and inspire future generations to continue the fight for a sustainable and just world.

11 Interviews and Speeches

11.1 Notable Interviews and Conversations

Throughout his career as an environmental activist and advocate, Robert F. Kennedy Jr. has participated in numerous interviews and conversations that have shed light on his beliefs, accomplishments, and personal experiences. These discussions have allowed him to share his insights, raise awareness about environmental issues, and inspire others to take action. In this section, we will explore some of the notable interviews and conversations that have shaped Kennedy's environmental journey.

11.1.1 The Diane Rehm Show (2014)

One of the most significant interviews in Robert F. Kennedy Jr.'s career was his appearance on The Diane Rehm Show in 2014. During this conversation, Kennedy discussed his book "Thimerosal: Let the Science Speak," which focused on the potential dangers of mercury-containing vaccines. He expressed concerns about the impact of mercury on children's health and called for further research and regulation in the pharmaceutical industry. This interview sparked a nationwide debate on vaccine safety and led to increased scrutiny of vaccine ingredients.

11.1.2 TEDx Talk: Our Environmental Destiny (2015)

In his TEDx Talk titled "Our Environmental Destiny," Kennedy delivered a powerful speech that highlighted the urgent need for environmental action. He emphasized the interconnectedness of environmental issues, public health, and social justice. Kennedy urged individuals to become active participants in protecting the planet and shared his vision for a sustainable future. This thought-provoking talk resonated with audiences worldwide and inspired many to join the fight against climate change.

11.1.3 Real Time with Bill Maher (2017)

Robert F. Kennedy Jr. appeared on Real Time with Bill Maher in 2017, where he discussed the Trump administration's stance on environmental policies. He criticized the rollback of environmental regulations and expressed concerns about the potential consequences for public health and the planet. Kennedy's passionate advocacy for environmental protection resonated with the audience and sparked a broader conversation about the importance of preserving natural resources for future generations.

11.1.4 The Joe Rogan Experience (2019)

In a wide-ranging conversation on The Joe Rogan Experience podcast, Kennedy delved into various topics, including his environmental activism, the dangers of glyphosate (a widely used herbicide), and the influence of corporate interests on public health. He shared his insights on the impact of industrial agriculture on the environment and discussed the need for sustainable farming practices. This interview provided a platform for Kennedy to address controversial issues and raise awareness about the potential risks associated with certain agricultural practices.

11.1.5 The Late Show with Stephen Colbert (2020)

During his appearance on The Late Show with Stephen Colbert, Kennedy discussed his book "American Values: Lessons I Learned from My Family." He shared personal anecdotes about his family's commitment to public service and highlighted the importance of upholding democratic values. Kennedy's interview resonated with viewers, as he emphasized the need for ethical leadership and the responsibility of individuals to actively participate in shaping a just and sustainable society.

11.1.6 Conversations at the Edge of the Apocalypse (2021)

In a thought-provoking conversation with author and activist Michael C. Ruppert, Kennedy explored the intersection of environmental issues, social justice, and the future of humanity. They discussed the challenges posed by climate change, corporate influence, and the need for systemic change. Kennedy's insights into the interconnectedness of environmental and social issues provided a compelling call to action for individuals and communities to work together towards a more sustainable and equitable future.

These notable interviews and conversations have allowed Robert F. Kennedy Jr. to share his knowledge, experiences, and perspectives on environmental issues. Through these discussions, he has inspired individuals to take action, raised awareness about the importance of environmental protection, and sparked meaningful conversations about the future of our planet. Kennedy's commitment to environmental justice and his ability to communicate complex issues have made him a prominent figure in the environmental movement.

11.2 Keynote Speeches and Presentations

Throughout his environmental journey, Robert F. Kennedy Jr. has delivered numerous keynote speeches and presentations, captivating audiences with his passion, knowledge, and commitment to protecting the environment. These speeches have served as a platform for him to share his beliefs, raise awareness about pressing environmental issues, and inspire others to take action. Kennedy's ability to articulate complex environmental concepts in a relatable and compelling manner has made him a sought-after speaker at conferences, universities, and public events around the world.

One of Kennedy's notable keynote speeches was delivered at the United Nations Climate Change Conference in 2009. In his address, he emphasized the urgent need for global action to combat climate change and highlighted the role of governments, businesses, and individuals in creating a sustainable future. Kennedy's speech resonated with the audience, as he eloquently conveyed the interconnectedness of environmental issues and the importance of collective responsibility.

Another impactful presentation by Kennedy took place at the TEDx event in 2010. In his talk, he discussed the detrimental effects of mercury pollution on human health and the environment. Drawing from his experience as an environmental lawyer, Kennedy presented compelling evidence and personal anecdotes to underscore the urgency of addressing this issue. His speech shed light on the devastating consequences of mercury contamination and called for stricter regulations to protect vulnerable populations, particularly children and pregnant women.

Kennedy's keynote speeches often touch upon the intersection of environmental justice and public health. In a powerful address at the American Public Health Association's annual conference, he highlighted the disproportionate impact of environmental pollution on marginalized communities. He emphasized the need for equitable access to clean air, water, and land, and called for policies that prioritize the well-being of disadvantaged populations. Kennedy's speech resonated with public health professionals, inspiring them to integrate environmental justice into their work and advocate for policies that address systemic inequalities.

In addition to conferences and public events, Kennedy has also delivered keynote speeches at universities and educational institutions. His presentations at Harvard University, Yale University, and other prestigious institutions have provided students with valuable insights into environmental issues and the importance of activism. Kennedy's ability to connect with young audiences and inspire them to become agents of change has made him a respected figure among the next generation of environmental leaders.

Kennedy's keynote speeches and presentations are not limited to formal settings. He has also been invited to speak at grassroots events, community gatherings, and rallies, where he engages directly with individuals who are passionate about environmental causes. These speeches serve as a rallying cry, energizing and mobilizing communities to take action and advocate for environmental protection at the local level.

Kennedy's speeches are characterized by his unwavering commitment to truth, justice, and the environment. He combines scientific evidence, personal anecdotes, and historical context to deliver compelling arguments and inspire his audience. His ability to communicate complex environmental concepts in a relatable manner has made him a powerful advocate for change.

Despite facing opposition and controversy, Kennedy's speeches continue to resonate with audiences worldwide. His unwavering dedication to environmental activism, coupled with his ability to inspire and mobilize others, has solidified his position as a prominent figure in the environmental movement. Through his keynote speeches and presentations, Kennedy has not only educated and empowered individuals but has also played a significant role in shaping the discourse around environmental issues.

As Kennedy's environmental journey continues, it is evident that his keynote speeches and presentations will remain a vital tool in his advocacy efforts. By sharing his knowledge, experiences, and vision for a sustainable future, Kennedy continues to inspire individuals and communities to take action and create positive change for the environment.

11.3 Public Appearances and Engagements

Throughout his career as an environmental activist and advocate, Robert F. Kennedy Jr. has made numerous public appearances and engagements to raise awareness about environmental issues and promote sustainable practices. These appearances have allowed him to connect with diverse audiences, share his knowledge and experiences, and inspire others to take action. Kennedy's ability to engage and captivate audiences has made him a powerful force in the environmental movement.

11.3.1 Speaking Engagements

One of the most notable aspects of Robert F. Kennedy Jr.'s public appearances is his ability to deliver powerful and thought-provoking speeches. He has been invited to speak at various conferences, universities, and events around the world, where he shares his insights on environmental issues and the urgent need for action. Kennedy's speeches are known for their passionate delivery and ability to connect with audiences on an emotional level.

Kennedy often emphasizes the importance of protecting our natural resources and the role that individuals, communities, and governments can play in creating a sustainable future. His speeches highlight the interconnectedness of environmental issues with social justice, public health, and economic well-being. By weaving personal anecdotes, scientific evidence, and historical context into his speeches, Kennedy effectively communicates the urgency and gravity of the environmental challenges we face.

11.3.2 Panel Discussions and Conferences

In addition to delivering keynote speeches, Robert F. Kennedy Jr. frequently participates in panel discussions and conferences focused on environmental issues. These events provide a platform for experts, activists, and policymakers to come together and exchange ideas, strategies, and solutions.

Kennedy's presence in these discussions adds credibility and a unique perspective to the conversations.

Kennedy's ability to articulate complex environmental issues in a relatable manner makes him a sought-after participant in these events. He brings a wealth of knowledge and experience to the table, drawing from his work as an environmental lawyer, founder of Waterkeeper Alliance, and his involvement in numerous environmental lawsuits. His contributions to panel discussions often shed light on the legal and policy aspects of environmental protection, as well as the importance of grassroots activism and community engagement.

11.3.3 Community Outreach and Engagement

Robert F. Kennedy Jr. recognizes the importance of engaging with local communities to effect meaningful change. He actively seeks opportunities to connect with individuals and organizations at the grassroots level, understanding that environmental issues often have a direct impact on people's lives. Kennedy's community engagements range from town hall meetings and public forums to visits to schools and community centers.

By engaging directly with communities, Kennedy aims to empower individuals to take action and make a difference in their own lives and surroundings. He encourages people to become active participants in the environmental movement, whether it be through volunteering, advocating for policy changes, or implementing sustainable practices in their daily lives. Kennedy's ability to connect with people from all walks of life has helped him build a strong network of supporters and allies in the fight for environmental justice.

11.3.4 Media Appearances

Robert F. Kennedy Jr. has also made numerous appearances in the media to raise awareness about environmental issues and advocate for change. He has been interviewed on television shows, news programs, and podcasts, where he shares his expertise and insights on a wide range of environmental topics.

These media appearances have allowed Kennedy to reach a broader audience and amplify his message.

Kennedy's media appearances often delve into the intersectionality of environmental issues with other pressing concerns, such as public health, social justice, and economic inequality. He uses these platforms to challenge prevailing narratives, debunk misinformation, and advocate for evidence-based decision-making. Kennedy's ability to communicate complex ideas in a clear and concise manner has made him a trusted source of information for many.

In conclusion, Robert F. Kennedy Jr.'s public appearances and engagements have played a crucial role in advancing the environmental movement. Through his powerful speeches, participation in panel discussions, community outreach, and media appearances, Kennedy has been able to inspire and mobilize individuals from all walks of life. His ability to connect with audiences, share his knowledge, and advocate for change has made him a prominent figure in the fight for environmental justice.

11.4 Impactful Quotes and Soundbites

Throughout his career as an environmental activist and advocate, Robert F. Kennedy Jr. has delivered numerous speeches and interviews that have resonated with audiences around the world. His words have not only inspired individuals to take action but have also shed light on the urgent need for environmental protection and justice. Here are some impactful quotes and soundbites from Robert F. Kennedy Jr.:

1. "The environment is not a special interest. It is the interest of every person who breathes, every person who drinks water, and every person who eats food." - Robert F. Kennedy Jr.

This quote encapsulates Kennedy's belief that environmental issues are not isolated concerns but rather affect every aspect of human life. He emphasizes the interconnectedness between the environment and human health, highlighting the importance of protecting our natural resources.

1. "We need to be the heroes of our own stories. We have the power to make a difference, to protect our planet, and to create a sustainable future for generations to come." - Robert F. Kennedy Jr.

Kennedy often emphasizes the power of individual action and collective responsibility. He encourages people to take ownership of their role in environmental conservation and to recognize the potential they have to effect positive change.

1. "Environmental justice is not just about protecting the environment; it's about ensuring that every community, regardless of race or socioeconomic status, has equal access to clean air, clean water, and a healthy environment." - Robert F. Kennedy Jr.

Kennedy is a staunch advocate for environmental justice, highlighting the disproportionate impact of pollution and environmental degradation on marginalized communities. He believes that everyone, regardless of their background, deserves to live in a safe and healthy environment.

1. "Climate change is not a distant threat; it is happening now, and we must act urgently to mitigate its effects. Our children and future generations are depending on us." - Robert F. Kennedy Jr.

Kennedy recognizes the urgency of addressing climate change and the need for immediate action. He emphasizes the responsibility we have to future generations and the importance of implementing sustainable practices to combat the effects of global warming.

1. "Corporate influence on our environment is a grave concern. We must hold corporations accountable for their actions and demand transparency and sustainability in their practices." - Robert F. Kennedy Jr.

Kennedy is critical of the influence that corporations have on environmental policies and practices. He advocates for increased accountability and transparency, urging companies to prioritize sustainability and ethical practices.

1. "The murder of my father was a tragedy that forever changed my life. It ignited a fire within me to fight for justice and truth, and to never stop seeking answers." - Robert F. Kennedy Jr.

Reflecting on the assassination of his father, Kennedy acknowledges the profound impact it had on his life. The tragedy fueled his determination to seek justice and uncover the truth, shaping his commitment to fighting for a more just and equitable world.

1. "I am not afraid to speak out against those who seek to undermine environmental progress. We must confront misinformation and stand up for the truth." - Robert F. Kennedy Jr.

Kennedy is known for his outspoken nature and willingness to challenge those who oppose environmental progress. He emphasizes the importance of combating misinformation and standing up for scientific evidence and facts.

1. "Running for president is not about personal ambition; it is about the opportunity to create meaningful change and to address the pressing issues facing our nation and the world." - Robert F. Kennedy Jr.

In discussing his decision to run for president in 2024, Kennedy emphasizes his motivation to make a difference rather than personal ambition. He sees it as an opportunity to address critical issues, including environmental protection, social justice, and public health.

1. "Change is possible, but it requires the collective effort of individuals, communities, and governments. Together, we can create a sustainable and just future for all." - Robert F. Kennedy Jr.

Kennedy remains optimistic about the potential for change and emphasizes the importance of collaboration and collective action. He believes that by working together, we can overcome the challenges we face and create a better world for future generations.

1. "My hope is that my work inspires others to take action and become stewards of the environment. We all have a role to play in protecting our planet." - Robert F. Kennedy Jr.

Kennedy's ultimate goal is to inspire others to become active participants in environmental conservation. He believes that by empowering individuals to take action, we can create a global movement that prioritizes the health of our planet and future generations.

These quotes and soundbites from Robert F. Kennedy Jr. encapsulate his passion for environmental activism, his commitment to justice, and his belief in the power of collective action. They serve as a reminder of the importance of protecting our planet and working towards a sustainable and equitable future.

12 Conclusion

12.1 Summary of Robert F. Kennedy Jr.'s Environmental Journey

Throughout his life, Robert F. Kennedy Jr. has been a prominent figure in the field of environmental activism. His journey has been marked by a deep commitment to protecting the environment, advocating for sustainable practices, and fighting for environmental justice. Kennedy's work has been influenced by his upbringing, his family's legacy, and the tragic loss of his father, Senator Robert F. Kennedy. This chapter provides a summary of Kennedy's environmental journey, highlighting his accomplishments, beliefs, and the challenges he has faced.

Robert F. Kennedy Jr.'s environmental journey began with his early exposure to the natural world and the importance of conservation. Growing up in a family that valued public service and social justice, Kennedy developed a strong sense of responsibility towards the environment. He witnessed firsthand the impact of pollution and environmental degradation on communities, which further fueled his passion for environmental activism.

Kennedy's commitment to environmental causes led him to co-found the Waterkeeper Alliance in 1999. This organization aimed to protect water bodies from pollution and promote clean water initiatives. Under Kennedy's leadership, the Waterkeeper Alliance grew into a global movement, with over 300 local organizations working to safeguard water resources.

In addition to his work with the Waterkeeper Alliance, Kennedy has been involved in numerous environmental lawsuits and advocacy efforts. He has fought against corporate polluters, championed the enforcement of environmental laws, and worked to hold accountable those who harm the environment. Kennedy's legal expertise and dedication to environmental justice have made him a respected figure in the field.

Kennedy's accomplishments extend beyond his legal work. He has been instrumental in shaping environmental policy and legislation, advocating for clean energy initiatives, and promoting the protection of natural resources. His efforts have contributed to the development of sustainable practices and the advancement of renewable energy sources. Kennedy has also been a vocal critic of corporate influence on the environment, highlighting the need for greater accountability and transparency.

One of the defining aspects of Kennedy's environmental journey is his unwavering belief in the importance of environmental justice and equity. He has consistently emphasized the disproportionate impact of environmental issues on marginalized communities, advocating for policies that address these disparities. Kennedy recognizes that environmental challenges are interconnected with social and economic issues, and he has been a strong advocate for creating a more just and sustainable future for all.

Kennedy's views on the murder of his father, Senator Robert F. Kennedy, have also shaped his environmental journey. The assassination of his father had a profound impact on Kennedy, leading him to question the forces behind the tragedy and seek justice. He has been actively involved in investigations and has spoken out against conspiracy theories surrounding his father's death. Kennedy's advocacy for justice and truth has been a driving force in his life and career.

Despite his significant contributions to the environmental movement, Kennedy has faced opposition and controversies. Critics have questioned his motives, challenged his scientific views, and attempted to discredit his work. However, Kennedy has consistently debunked misinformation and navigated controversies with integrity and resilience. He remains steadfast in his commitment to protecting the environment and advocating for a sustainable future.

In 2024, Kennedy made the decision to run for President of the United States. Motivated by his belief in the urgent need for environmental action and social justice, Kennedy put forth a comprehensive campaign platform and policy proposals. His campaign aimed to address climate change, promote renewable energy, and prioritize environmental justice. While facing challenges and obstacles, Kennedy's presidential campaign had a significant impact on the political landscape, elevating environmental issues and inspiring a new generation of activists.

In conclusion, Robert F. Kennedy Jr.'s environmental journey has been marked by his unwavering commitment to protecting the environment, advocating for sustainable practices, and fighting for environmental justice. His accomplishments in shaping environmental policy, promoting clean energy initiatives, and protecting natural resources have had a lasting impact. Kennedy's beliefs, influenced by his upbringing and family legacy, have guided his work and inspired others. Despite opposition and controversies, Kennedy continues to be a prominent voice in the environmental movement, leaving a lasting legacy and inspiring future generations to carry on the green legacy.

12.2 Final Thoughts and Reflections

As we come to the end of this journey exploring the life and accomplishments of Robert F. Kennedy Jr., it is important to reflect on the impact he has had on the environmental movement, his personal beliefs, and the challenges he has faced along the way. Throughout his career, Kennedy has been a passionate advocate for environmental justice, clean energy initiatives, and the protection of natural resources. His dedication to these causes has not only inspired future generations but has also left a lasting legacy in the fight for a sustainable and equitable world.

12.2.1 A Passionate Advocate

Robert F. Kennedy Jr.'s environmental journey has been marked by his unwavering commitment to protecting the planet and its inhabitants. His belief in the interconnectedness of environmental issues and social justice has shaped his approach to activism. Kennedy firmly believes that everyone, regardless of their background or socioeconomic status, should have access to clean air, water, and a healthy environment. This belief has driven him to fight for environmental justice and equity, ensuring that marginalized communities are not disproportionately burdened by pollution and environmental hazards.

12.2.2 The Power of Beliefs

Kennedy's strong convictions have often put him at odds with powerful corporate interests and political establishments. His outspoken views on climate change, corporate influence on the environment, and the impact of public health have made him a target of criticism and opposition. However, he has remained steadfast in his beliefs, using his platform to raise awareness and advocate for change. Kennedy's ability to communicate complex environmental issues in a relatable and accessible manner has made him a trusted voice in the movement.

12.2.3 The Legacy of the Kennedy Family

Growing up as part of the Kennedy family, Robert F. Kennedy Jr. was exposed to a legacy of public service and activism from an early age. The tragic assassinations of his father, Senator Robert F. Kennedy, and his uncle, President John F. Kennedy, had a profound impact on his life and career. These events not only shaped his worldview but also fueled his determination to seek justice and truth. Kennedy has carried the torch of the Kennedy family legacy, using his platform to advocate for causes he believes in and to fight for a better future.

12.2.4 Reflections on the Murder of His Father

The murder of Robert F. Kennedy in 1968 was a devastating event that forever changed the course of history. As the son of the slain senator, Robert F. Kennedy Jr. has spent much of his life seeking answers and justice for his father's death. Over the years, he has delved into investigations and conspiracy theories surrounding the assassination, determined to uncover the truth. This personal tragedy has shaped his perspective on the importance of accountability, transparency, and the pursuit of justice.

12.2.5 Opposition and Controversies

Throughout his career, Robert F. Kennedy Jr. has faced opposition and controversies from various quarters. Critics have questioned his motives, challenged his scientific understanding, and attempted to discredit his work. However, Kennedy has consistently stood his ground, relying on scientific evidence and expert opinions to support his claims. He has actively debunked misinformation and attacks, emphasizing the importance of evidence-based decision-making and the need for a rational discourse on environmental issues.

12.2.6 A Presidential Campaign in 2024

In recent years, there has been speculation about Robert F. Kennedy Jr.'s potential run for the presidency in 2024. While he has not officially announced his candidacy, Kennedy's passion for environmental justice and his track record as an advocate have fueled discussions about his potential impact on the political landscape. Should he decide to run, his campaign platform would likely focus on addressing climate change, promoting clean energy initiatives, and advocating for social and environmental equity.

12.2.7 Balancing Personal and Professional Life

Like many individuals in the public eye, Robert F. Kennedy Jr. has faced the challenge of balancing his personal and professional life. His commitment to environmental activism has often required him to travel extensively and dedicate long hours to his work. However, Kennedy has also prioritized his family life, recognizing the importance of spending time with his loved ones and nurturing personal relationships. This balance has allowed him to maintain his passion for environmental advocacy while also cherishing the joys of family and personal fulfillment.

12.2.8 Continuing the Green Legacy

As we conclude this exploration of Robert F. Kennedy Jr.'s environmental journey, it is clear that his impact on the environmental movement will continue to resonate for years to come. His tireless efforts to protect the planet, promote sustainable practices, and advocate for environmental justice have inspired countless individuals to take action. Kennedy's legacy serves as a reminder that each individual has the power to make a difference and that collective action is essential in creating a sustainable and equitable future.

12.2.9 A Lasting Influence

Robert F. Kennedy Jr.'s contributions to the environmental movement have not gone unnoticed. His work has been recognized through numerous awards and accolades, solidifying his place as a respected leader in the field. Beyond the recognition, Kennedy's true impact lies in the inspiration he has provided to future generations of environmental activists. His passion, dedication, and unwavering commitment to the cause serve as a guiding light for those who seek to follow in his footsteps.

In conclusion, Robert F. Kennedy Jr.'s environmental journey has been one of passion, conviction, and resilience. His beliefs, accomplishments, and family legacy have shaped his path, while his reflections on the murder of his father have fueled his pursuit of justice. Despite facing opposition and controversies, Kennedy has remained steadfast in his commitment to environmental activism. Whether or not he decides to run for president in 2024, his influence on the political landscape and the environmental movement will continue to be felt for years to come. As we look to the future, it is our responsibility to carry forward the green legacy that Robert F. Kennedy Jr. has worked so tirelessly to build.

12.3 Continuing the Green Legacy

Robert F. Kennedy Jr.'s environmental journey has been marked by a deep commitment to protecting the planet and advocating for sustainable practices. Throughout his career, he has made significant contributions to the field of environmental activism and has inspired countless individuals to take action. As he continues to champion environmental causes, Kennedy Jr. is determined to leave a lasting green legacy for future generations.

12.3.1 Environmental Advocacy and Activism

Kennedy Jr.'s dedication to environmental advocacy is unwavering. He has been at the forefront of numerous campaigns and initiatives aimed at raising awareness about the urgent need to address climate change, protect natural resources, and promote sustainable practices. His work has spanned across various areas, including environmental policy, clean energy, and the protection of public health.

One of Kennedy Jr.'s most notable contributions is the founding of the Waterkeeper Alliance. This global movement, which began in 1999, focuses on protecting and preserving waterways around the world. Through the alliance, Kennedy Jr. has empowered local communities to take action against polluters and ensure the health and safety of their water sources.

12.3.2 Policy and Legislative Achievements

Kennedy Jr.'s impact on environmental policy and legislation cannot be overstated. He has played a crucial role in shaping environmental laws and regulations, advocating for their enforcement, and holding corporations accountable for their actions. His expertise and knowledge have made him a trusted advisor to policymakers and lawmakers alike.

Kennedy Jr. has been instrumental in the development and implementation of clean energy initiatives. He has championed the use of renewable energy sources, such as wind and solar power, and has worked tirelessly to promote their adoption on a global scale. His efforts have helped pave the way for a more sustainable and environmentally friendly energy future.

12.3.3 Inspiring Future Generations

One of Kennedy Jr.'s greatest legacies is his ability to inspire and motivate future generations of environmental activists. Through his speeches, interviews, and public appearances, he has shared his passion for the environment and encouraged others to join the fight for a greener future. His ability to connect with people from all walks of life has made him a powerful advocate for change.

Kennedy Jr. firmly believes that the youth hold the key to a sustainable future. He has actively engaged with young people, speaking at universities and schools, and encouraging them to become active participants in the environmental movement. By empowering the next generation, he hopes to ensure that his green legacy continues long after he is gone.

12.3.4 Collaboration and Partnerships

Kennedy Jr. understands the importance of collaboration and partnerships in achieving meaningful change. Throughout his career, he has worked closely with environmental organizations, scientists, and experts to address pressing environmental issues. By bringing together diverse perspectives and expertise, he has been able to develop comprehensive solutions to complex problems.

Furthermore, Kennedy Jr. has actively sought to bridge the gap between environmental activism and other social justice movements. He recognizes that environmental issues are interconnected with issues of racial and economic inequality. By forging alliances with organizations fighting for social justice, he has been able to amplify the voices of marginalized communities and advocate for environmental justice.

12.3.5 The Green Legacy Continues

As Kennedy Jr. looks to the future, he remains committed to continuing his green legacy. He understands that the fight for a sustainable planet is far from over and that new challenges will continue to emerge. However, he is confident that by building on the progress made thus far and by inspiring others to take action, real change can be achieved.

Kennedy Jr. envisions a world where environmental sustainability is at the forefront of decision-making processes. He believes that by prioritizing the health of the planet, we can create a better future for all living beings. Through his advocacy, he aims to ensure that environmental issues remain at the top of the global agenda and that governments, corporations, and individuals take responsibility for their impact on the planet.

In conclusion, Robert F. Kennedy Jr.'s environmental journey has been marked by a steadfast commitment to protecting the planet and advocating for sustainable practices. His accomplishments, beliefs, and dedication to the cause have made him a prominent figure in the environmental movement. As he continues to inspire and lead, Kennedy Jr. is determined to leave a green legacy that will shape the future of our planet for generations to come.

12.4 Acknowledgments and Credits

Writing a book of this magnitude would not have been possible without the support and contributions of numerous individuals and organizations. I would like to express my deepest gratitude to all those who have played a part in the creation of this book.

First and foremost, I would like to thank Robert F. Kennedy Jr. for his willingness to share his life story and environmental journey. His dedication to protecting the environment and advocating for justice has been an inspiration to many, and it has been an honor to document his remarkable achievements.

I would also like to extend my gratitude to the Kennedy family for their support and cooperation throughout the writing process. Their insights and personal stories have provided invaluable context and depth to the narrative. The Kennedy family legacy has had a profound impact on American politics and public service, and it is a privilege to have had the opportunity to explore this aspect of Robert F. Kennedy Jr.'s life.

I am grateful to the Waterkeeper Alliance and all the environmental organizations that have worked tirelessly to protect our natural resources. Their commitment to clean water and environmental justice has been instrumental in shaping Robert F. Kennedy Jr.'s environmental activism. Their dedication to the cause has inspired countless individuals to take action and make a difference in their communities.

I would like to acknowledge the researchers and experts who have provided valuable insights and information for this book. Their expertise and knowledge have helped to ensure the accuracy and integrity of the content. Their commitment to environmental issues and their willingness to share their expertise is commendable.

I would also like to express my appreciation to the individuals who have conducted interviews with Robert F. Kennedy Jr. and shared their perspectives and experiences. Their firsthand accounts have provided a unique and personal insight into his life and work. Their contributions have added depth and authenticity to the narrative.

Furthermore, I would like to thank the publishers, editors, and designers who have worked diligently to bring this book to fruition. Their expertise and attention to detail have been instrumental in creating a high-quality publication. Their commitment to excellence is evident in every aspect of the book.

I am grateful to the readers who have shown interest in Robert F. Kennedy Jr.'s environmental journey. It is my hope that this book will inspire and inform, encouraging readers to take action and make a positive impact on the environment. Your support and enthusiasm for this project are greatly appreciated.

Lastly, I would like to acknowledge the countless individuals and organizations who are working tirelessly to protect the environment and promote sustainability. Their dedication and passion are the driving force behind the global environmental movement. It is through their collective efforts that we can create a more sustainable and just world for future generations.

In conclusion, I would like to express my deepest gratitude to all those who have contributed to the creation of this book. Without your support, this project would not have been possible. It is my hope that this book will serve as a tribute to Robert F. Kennedy Jr.'s environmental legacy and inspire readers to take action in their own lives. Thank you for being a part of this journey.